inside
tennis

inside tennis

stan smith

with
tom valentine

HENRY REGNERY COMPANY・CHICAGO

Copyright © 1974 by Stan Smith and Tom Valentine.
All rights reserved.
Published by Henry Regnery Company
180 North Michigan Avenue, Chicago, Illinois 60601
Manufactured in the United States of America
Library of Congress Catalog Card Number: 73-20692
International Standard Book Number: 0-8092-8887-7 (cloth)
0-8092-8886-9 (paper)

PHOTO CREDITS
Cover photo: Edward Fernberger
Pages 68, 70, 73: Russ Adams
All other photos by Morton Broffman

introduction

People have been playing games related to tennis since the Middle Ages. Early in the fourteenth century, French knights introduced aristocratic Europeans to *court tennis,* a game played by hitting a small, stuffed ball over a net with a rough, handmade racket. The game was played on enclosed indoor courts. Court tennis was a favorite sport of such princes as Henry VIII. Louis XIV had tennis courts built at Versailles, and it was on one of Louis XIV's courts that the Tennis Court Oath was signed at the beginning of the French Revolution.

Although the ancient game of court tennis is still played today, what most people think of as "tennis" is the modern game, *lawn tennis,* which was introduced in England in 1873. Major Walter Wingfield of the British Army published a pamphlet describing a game he called *sphairistike* (Greek for "play ball"). The new game soon replaced croquet as England's most popular lawn sport.

Tennis was brought to the United States in 1874, and the first national championships were held on the lawn of the Newport Casino in 1887. In 1900 a young Harvard student, Dwight Davis, got the idea for an international tennis competition, and the rivalry for the Davis Cup began.

For a long time, tennis was a "gentleman's game," associated in the popular mind with the leisure class. Such major tournaments as Wimbledon were open only to amateurs. Although professional tennis players could not compete at the world's most prestigious tournaments, the so-called "amateur" players often received expense money that allowed them to play. The situation caused a great deal of frustration among the pros. The conflict was eliminated in 1968, when the major tournaments decided to eliminate the distinction between amateur and pro and offer prize money to attract more pros. Since that year, the year of "open tennis," the sport has been booming. What the game lost in snob appeal it has gained in popularity. New indoor and outdoor courts are being built all over the country. Over 10 million Americans now play tennis, and the number is increasing every day.

The widespread public enthusiasm for tennis has been a major factor in the dramatic changes taking place in the sport. More tennis championships are being shown on prime-time television. New scoring rules are being tested that will make the games shorter and more exciting for spectators.

More big changes are happening in women's pro tennis. In 1970, together with Gladys Heldman, publisher of *World Tennis,* a group of professional woman players formed their own tour, the Virginia Slims circuit. The women had complained about receiving too small a share of the prize money in tournaments that featured both men and women. Now the Virginia Slims players are drawing capacity crowds and top money, and, what is perhaps more important, more women all over the United States are beginning to play tennis.

As for myself, I think I've been lucky in coming to tennis at a time when so much is happening in the sport. I started playing tennis when I was in high school—a little later than most pros begin. Before that I played several different sports, with basketball, baseball, and football being my favorites. Early in my tennis career, Pancho Segura, one of the all-time great players, became my instructor and patron. Pancho has some of the smartest tactics in tennis—what he taught me about strategy has helped put me on top.

The rewards of being on top in tennis are many—money, the fun of travel, the thrill of competing against the world's greatest players. But it's a taxing life, too. Tennis demands concentration, practice, and constant conditioning.

I hope to pass on to you some of what I've learned. I'll deal with all the mechanics of the game, from serving to volleying. I'll talk about strategy, about winning tactics, and about playing under various conditions. Whether you are just starting out in tennis or whether you've been playing for years, I know I can help you improve. Above all, I hope I can communicate my own enjoyment of tennis. I fight hard to win, and it's a great feeling to be a champion. But my real reason for playing is that I love the game. If you approach tennis with that attitude, you'll come out ahead.

Stan Smith

contents

	Introduction	1
1	Before You Begin	5
2	The Serve	15
3	The Basic Strokes	31
4	Playing the Game	43
5	Winning Tactics	61
6	Doubles	69
7	Practice and Conditioning	77
	Glossary	85
	Index	89

QUICK EXCHANGES AT THE NET . . . characterize the modern, aggressive tennis game. Developing the kind of serve and volley game the pros play takes years of practice and dedication.

chapter 1
BEFORE YOU BEGIN

Before you go out on the tennis court and start practicing, let's review the basics of the game. In *singles* tennis, two players stand on opposite sides of a net, which is strung across a court. The players hit the ball back and forth until one player hits the ball into the net or out of bounds or fails to return the ball. The other player then scores a point. In doubles tennis, there are two players on each side of the net.

The rules of tennis are interpreted and enforced by the International Lawn Tennis Federation (ILTF), of which the United States Lawn Tennis Association (USLTA) is a member. Tennis rules are quite simple, and I will be telling you about most of them in this chapter. If you need more information, you can get a copy of USLTA rules at any large sporting goods store. Or, write to:

United States Lawn Tennis Association
51 East 42nd Street
New York, New York 10017

THE COURT

All tennis courts, regardless of their composition, are the same size. Court dimensions are established by the ILTF. These dimensions are shown in Diagram 1.

There are two different boundaries on a tennis court. The narrow boundary is used for singles play, while the wider boundary is used for doubles. The area between the two boundaries is known as the *alley*.

Each side of the tennis court is divided into a *forecourt* and a *backcourt*. The forecourt is divided into left and right *service courts*. The ball may be hit anywhere in the forecourt or backcourt, except on the serve, when it must be hit into the correct service court. Balls hit on the line are considered *in bounds*.

Court Surfaces

As the name "lawn tennis" implies, tennis was originally played on grass.

6 BEFORE YOU BEGIN

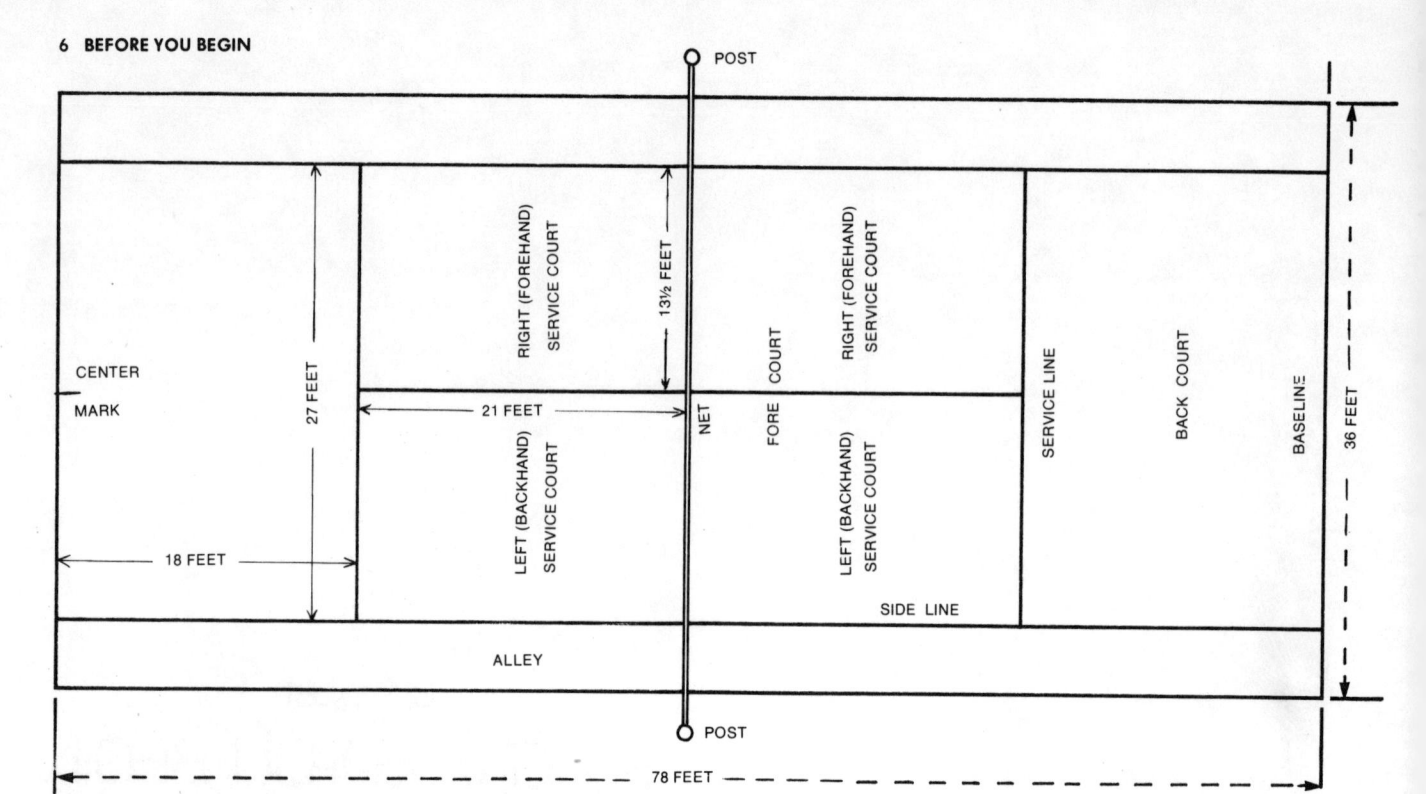

DIAGRAM 1. The dimensions of the tennis court.

Although Wimbledon and other major tournaments are still played on grass, the days of the grass court are numbered. One reason is that the upkeep needed to keep grass courts in perfect condition is incredible—and nowadays it's just too expensive. Grass absorbs moisture quickly and dries slowly. The ball doesn't bounce very high on grass, and this makes the game much faster. Of course, grass is easy on the feet, but because it's so slippery it can also be treacherous.

Clay is a slow surface. The ball bounces higher on clay, but you still have to plan your shots very carefully. Like grass, clay is a slippery surface, and the ball doesn't always bounce evenly on it.

A lot of public tennis courts are made of cement or concrete. These courts provide a faster, harder game if they are smooth and a slower, more erratic game if they are rough. This surface is pretty tough on your feet.

I think the future of tennis lies with the new synthetic courts. There are many brands available now—Grasstex, Dynaturf, Laykold, Plexipave, Sportface, Astroturf, and Uniturf, to name just a few. These surfaces vary widely in composition. Sportface, for example, is a carpetlike fiber surface that is installed over a sub-base. Uniturf is a rubber surface, while Dynaturf is made of plastic.

Synthetic court surfaces require little maintenance. They dry quickly after rain. They are cleaner than clay and easier on the feet than concrete courts, and they provide a firmer footing than clay or grass courts. Surfaces such as Sportface provide a true bounce—no more of the crazy skidding and bouncing that is so common on the older surfaces. Synthetic courts remove a large element of chance from the game.

The synthetic surfaces are gradually taking over tennis, although we'll have other surfaces for many years to come. One proof of this trend is that the famous

Longwood Cricket Club in Boston, site of the United States Professional Men's Tournament and long a holdout for grass courts, is now using some synthetic courts for tournament play.

Indoor Courts

The tennis boom has also created a building boom. Indoor courts are turning tennis into a year-round sport. Most of these indoor courts have synthetic surfaces as well as controlled temperature, humidity, and lighting. Good indoor courts remove even more of the elements of chance from tennis.

EQUIPMENT

Tennis equipment should be chosen carefully, and with all the fancy equipment available, it's sometimes hard for a novice to know how to choose. Let me give you some hints before you start spending money.

The Racket

The conversation in the lounge at any

THE RIGHT TENNIS RACKET... is extremely important, and there is a wide selection available for players of varying abilities. I use a racket manufactured by Wilson Sporting Goods.

tennis club will invariably come around to the subject of the best racket material. A lot of medium to advanced players prefer the newer metal rackets to the older wood ones. Metal rackets provide more power, are lighter in weight, and are usually more flexible. Wood rackets, on the other hand, usually provide greater control.

Use the type of racket that's most comfortable for you. If you're a beginner, I'd suggest you start with wood until you've mastered the game and learned to place and control the ball. Then you might want to experiment with other materials.

I prefer to use a wood racket, even though I get more power with a metal one. The wood allows me finer control—and to me that's more important than power.

There are some other factors you should consider in choosing a racket—*weight, grip,* and *balance.*

Tennis rackets vary in weight from about 12 ounces to 15 ounces or more. If you use a racket that's too heavy for you, it will slow down your game. But a racket that's too light won't give you enough power. Play with the heaviest racket that you can handle comfortably. The racket I use weighs 14½ ounces when strung. That's a fairly heavy racket, but I play a lot of tennis and keep up my game. An occasional player may need a lighter racket—about 14 ounces is average for male players of average size and strength. Women usually use lighter rackets.

The handle, or *grip,* of a racket comes in standard sizes—4½, 4⅝, 4¾, and 4⅞ inches. I use a 4⅞-inch grip because of my large hands. Again, use the largest size that you can handle comfortably. The handle can be made of wood or plastic covered with leather.

A good tennis racket is balanced properly. A racket that is too heavy in the *head* (the top of the racket) will be hard to control. The standard test for weight distribution is to put your finger under the *throat* of the racket, the spot where the handle joins the head, and try to balance the racket. The racket should balance horizontally. A racket that concentrates the weight in the lower half of the head will be easier to manipulate than one that is top-heavy.

When you buy a racket, it will usually be unstrung. How tight you have it strung will affect the kind of game you play, and vice versa. Obviously, a tightly strung racket will hit the ball harder, but if it's too tight the handle will vibrate when you hit the ball and you'll lose control. A loosely strung racket slows down the ball. Most good players have the racket strung with about 60 pounds of pressure. If the racket is strung with *gut,* humidity will loosen the strings and dry air will tighten them, so it's best to test the racket frequently. If you have a wood racket, you should keep it in a *press* so that it won't warp.

There's certainly no need to buy an expensive racket if you're just starting out, but neither should you use poor-quality equipment. Your club pro or the proprietor at your local tennis shop will be glad to help you select exactly what you need.

Balls

Tennis balls must meet rigid ILTF requirements for size, weight, and rebound. Buy good-quality balls from a well-known manufacturer, and buy new balls often. Open a new can of balls for every important match, and make sure the ones you're using have retained their nap and bounce. Don't throw the old

TENNIS CLOTHES SHOULD STRETCH... to allow complete freedom of movement on those hard-to-reach shots. The new drip-dry synthetic fabrics are ideal.

balls away, though—they're fine for practicing serves and other shots.

Traditionally, tennis balls were white —that is, until the color of the court (green for grass, red or brown for clay) rubbed off on them. Balls are now being manufactured in bright colors that are easier to see on the newer synthetic courts. In tournaments, either white or yellow balls may be used.

Clothing

Like tennis balls, tennis clothing was traditionally white—in fact, until recently it was improper to appear on the court in any other color. Television coverage of tennis has changed all that—we pros now wear colored clothing so that television audiences can tell us apart. Although white remains the favorite, tennis fashions now come in many shades.

Your clothes should be loose fitting, comfortable, and easy to care for. The new drip-dry synthetic fabrics make it easy to present an attractive appearance with very little fuss. Your clothes must allow you room to bend and stretch. If you have long hair, you'll need some sort of band to keep it out of your eyes.

Your tennis shoes should have thick, comfortable soles with plenty of grip. There are many good brands on the market. Buy shoes large enough so that you can wear two pairs of socks to ab-

YOUR TENNIS SHOES... must have good soles and should provide support for all the sudden starts and stops on a variety of surfaces.

sorb sweat and cushion your feet. Don't wear your shoes for too long—all those quick stops and starts can really wear down the rubber, and a smooth sole on a slippery surface can be dangerous.

In humid or hot weather, a sweatband for your wrist can make all the difference in your game. If you're playing in the sun, wearing a hat can help a lot. I sometimes dip a handkerchief in water and wrap it around my neck while I'm playing to help me keep cool. I keep my feet dry by wearing two pairs of socks and changing them in between matches.

HOW TO PLAY THE GAME

Now that you're dressed and ready, let me tell you how a tennis game is played. You should begin playing games soon after you have developed your basic strokes—that way, you'll learn to use your skills in competitive situations.

A game of tennis begins with a *serve* from the right side of the court to the opponent's right side. The opponent must return the serve after the ball has bounced once. Play continues until one player misses the ball or hits it into the net or out of bounds.

Players may hit the ball before it bounces or after it has bounced once. If a ball bounces twice in a player's court, that player loses the point.

At the end of the first game the second player becomes the server. The players alternate serves until one player wins a *set*. The players must change sides after the first, third, and every subsequent alternate game of a set. They also change sides at the end of a set unless they have played an even number of games. In that case, they change sides after the first game of the second set.

SCORING

If you've been following tennis at all,

you know that scoring is another area of big change in the game. Traditional scoring, which is still used in USLTA tournaments, is *15-30-40-game.* In other words, the first point is called 15, the second is called 30, and the third 40. The first player who makes four points wins, unless the score is tied at 40-40. The score is then called *deuce.* The next point scored after deuce is called *advantage,* or ad. If the player who wins the advantage wins the succeeding point, he wins the game. Otherwise, the score is once again deuce. Under traditional rules, a game can last almost indefinitely, until one player has won by two points. When the losing player fails to score any points, his score is called *love.*

In spite of the illogical numbering, this scoring system is really very simple. A game is won by the first player who wins four points or wins by two.

Similarly, in traditional tennis, a *set* is won by the first player to win six games by at least two games. In other words, you can win a set 6-4, but not 6-5. If the score were 6-5, you'd have to play one more game, to win by 7-5. If your opponent won instead, tying the score at 6-6, you'd have to play at least two more games, to win 8-6. A *match* consists of three or five sets.

As you can see, under this system a match could last almost forever, and on several notable occasions the system has worn out both players and spectators. In 1967 a doubles match (Len Schloss and Tom Mozur vs. Dick Dell and Dick Leach) lasted six hours before Dell and Leach finally won 3-6, 49-47, 22-20. This interminable play might have been okay in the days before timed, television matches, but now it's become apparent that some method of shortening play has to be used.

The man responsible for many of the changes in scoring is James Henry Van Alen, founder of *VASSS* (Van Alen Simplified Scoring System). VASSS still hasn't been accepted entirely, but one form of it is now in use: the tie-breaker. In 1972 the USLTA sanctioned use of two forms of the tie-breaker. The tie-breakers are used after the score is tied at 6-6. One form, the 12-point, is used by the World Championship of Tennis Circuit and several other big tournaments. Under this system, the first player to score seven points wins, unless the score is tied at 6-6, in which case the first player to establish a margin of 2 points wins. The serve changes every two points except after a 6-6 tie, when it changes on every point.

A much faster—and much more deadly—tie-breaker is the 9-point, or *Sudden Death,* a phrase that brings chills to most professional players. When one point makes the difference between winning and losing a national title and, say, $20,000, you learn what it's really like to be nervous.

Imagine this situation: You've played for 3½ hours and have won two sets and six games apiece. You play the tie-breaker to four points all. Now it's the *match point* for both players. It's your serve, but you miss your first shot. There are few situations in pro sports that are so full of tension. The gallery is utterly silent. You serve, he returns, you rush to the net and cut off the shot, and it's over, just that fast. The Sudden-Death tie-breaker is often called the heartbreaker, because the loser has come so close to victory and has seen it slip away.

The VASSS system proposed several other ways to change tennis scoring. One way would be to score tennis like table tennis, with the serve changing every five points. Another system is the

SPECTATORS SHOULD REMAIN SILENT... during crucial moments of play when the player needs to concentrate on his strokes. Of course, applause is welcome after the point has been completed.

no-ad, in which the seventh point is always the last. The no-ad system has been experimented with in tournament play, but it is a long way from being accepted by the USLTA.

Whatever happens with the scoring, I think tennis will continue in the direction it's now taking. Games will be shorter and faster and competition will be more fierce. The game is well on its way to being the most exciting spectator sport around.

CONDUCT

Mostly because of its reputation as a "gentleman's sport," tennis has evolved a fairly complicated system of etiquette. Some of these unwritten rules—such as dressing all in white—are changing, but I hope the unwritten rules of courtesy and sportsmanship won't change.

A good tennis player will refrain from calling out or distracting his opponent during the serve. He will also refrain from making disparaging comments at any time. He won't dawdle unnecessarily during a time out. He won't disturb players on another court either, but will wait until their play stops before retrieving a ball.

In a game where there are no referees, a player must call all the shots that land on his side. Always give your opponent the benefit of the doubt on close or line shots. If there is serious disagreement, the shot should be played over.

If you are a spectator, try to maintain silence while the ball is in play, especially during a serve. Avoid making catcalls, booing, or yelling distracting things at either player while the point is being played—of course, cheer and applaud your favorite after the point is over. Don't run behind a court while the ball is in play.

If you have reserved a court at your local tennis club, show up on time and vacate the court on time. Some public courts use a racking system to reserve courts. Never take advantage of the system by switching rackets or otherwise barging ahead in line. As you can see, most of the "unwritten rules" of tennis are simply rules of common courtesy.

Whenever I see my opponent getting upset and using unsportsmanlike tactics, I assume his concentration is slipping and he's getting nervous. I try to keep my cool and concentrate—and that's why I perform well under pressure. After all, in the final analysis, it is not the player who screams and yells more or less who wins—it is the player who has the better control of himself and his game.

A STRONG, CONSISTENT SERVE . . . is the key to success in match play and can be a deadly offensive weapon. A professional tennis player counts on winning all the games he serves.

chapter 2
THE SERVE

Your serve is the most important shot in your tennis game. On your serve, you are the only one in control of the ball. A player who has a consistent, strong serve puts his opponent on the defensive right from the start. A poor server ends up losing most of his games because he serves the ball into the net or out of bounds.

RULES FOR SERVING

In order to serve, a player must stand behind the baseline, between the center mark and the sideline. His feet must not cross the baseline until after contact is made with the ball; if they do, a *foot fault* is called.

The server must hit the ball from the proper side of the court. The first serve of a game is hit from the right, or forehand, side, *crosscourt* into the service court on the opponent's right side (Diagram 2). Each time a point is scored, the server moves to the other side to serve. The second point, in other words, is served from the left, or backhand, side to the receiver's left service court. A served ball must land in the proper service court or a *fault* is called. The service court is the same for doubles and singles.

If a player faults on his first serve of a point, he is allowed a second serve. If he misses the second serve, he commits a *double fault* and his opponent scores a point.

A serve that hits the net and then bounces into the proper service court is called a *let ball* and is served over.

FUNDAMENTALS OF SERVING

I'm going to show you how to master the basic serves—the *flat serve,* the *slice serve,* and the *American twist serve.* First, however, let's look at the parts of any successful serve.

16 THE SERVE

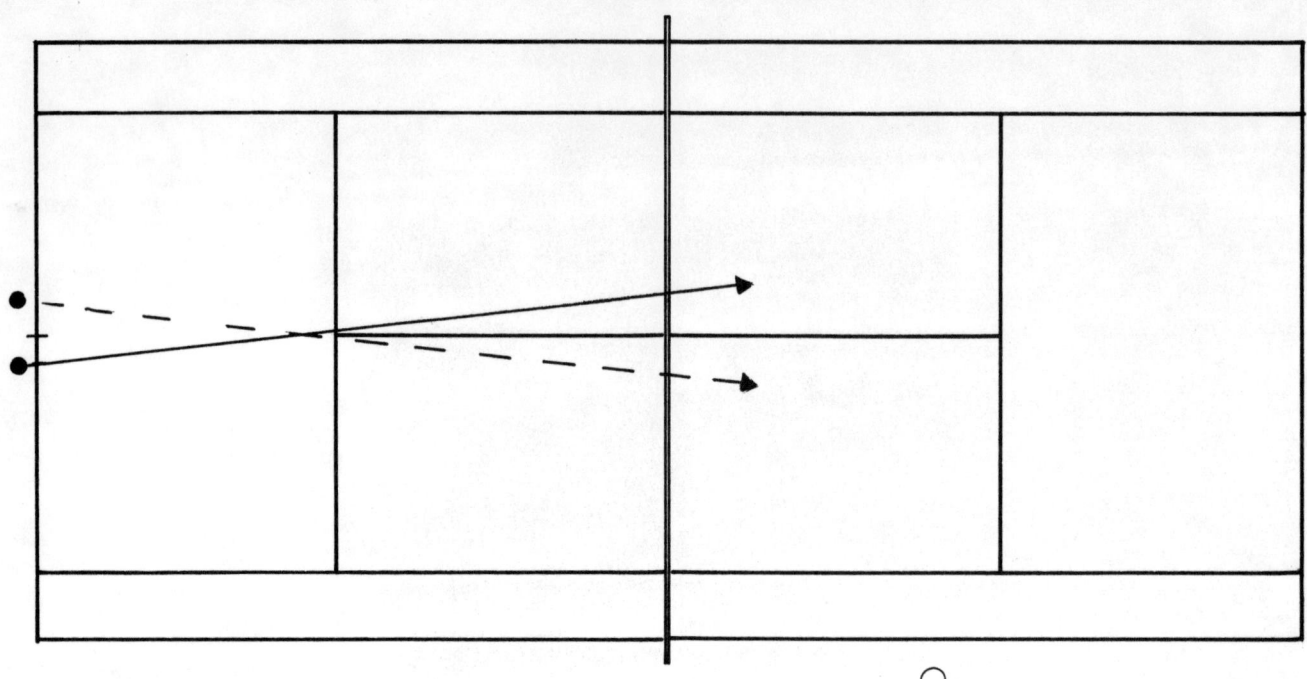

DIAGRAM 2. Correct placement of the serve.

**DIAGRAM 3.
The parts of a serve.**

THE CONTINENTAL GRIP...
is a backhand grip that is
also used in serving.

Grip

The grip on the serve is difficult for some beginning and intermediate players to understand. Most beginners should use the *Eastern,* or *forehand,* grip on the serve. The forehand grip is found by "shaking hands" with the racket, with the thumb and forefinger forming a "V" on top of the racket. This grip is fine for returning serve on the forehand side—in fact, in a later chapter, I'll be showing you how to use the forehand grip. Use it to serve when you first begin to get the feel of getting the ball into the service court, but not forever.

The correct grip for serving is the

18 THE SERVE

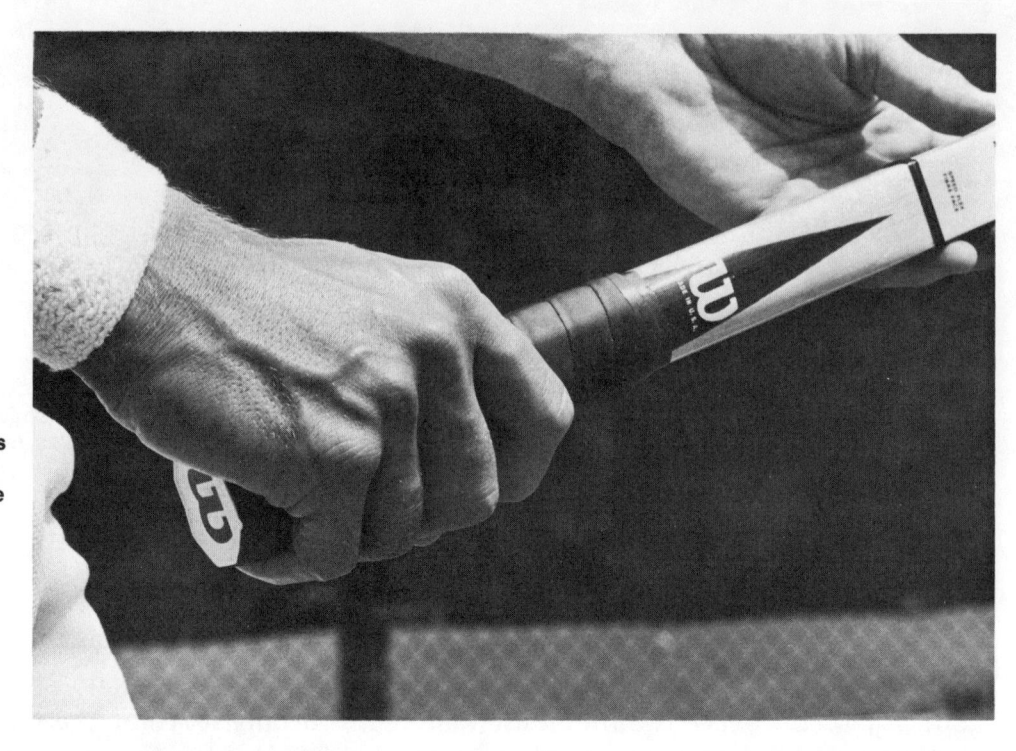

SPREADING YOUR FINGERS ... covers more of the handle and gives you more control of your strokes.

Continental grip, which is reached by moving the hand one eighth of a turn toward the left from the forehand grip. This slight turn is necessary to provide more strength during the motion of the backswing. When you grip the racket, spread your fingers slightly to cover more of the handle and give more control.

Stance

Begin your serve by standing with your feet at about a 45-degree angle to the baseline. If you are right-handed, your left foot should be the one nearest the baseline; if you are left-handed, your right foot should be the one in front. It is usually best to place your front foot about one or two inches behind the line. Your feet should be about shoulders' width apart. If you place your feet almost parallel to the baseline, so that your body is almost at a right angle to the line, you will get more spin on your serve.

The Toss

Try to imagine a ball that is suspended at exactly the right spot for each serve. A perfect *toss* will accomplish this, so it pays to practice your toss until you get it right where you want it.

To begin the toss, hold the ball with your first three fingers and support it with your thumb and little finger. The

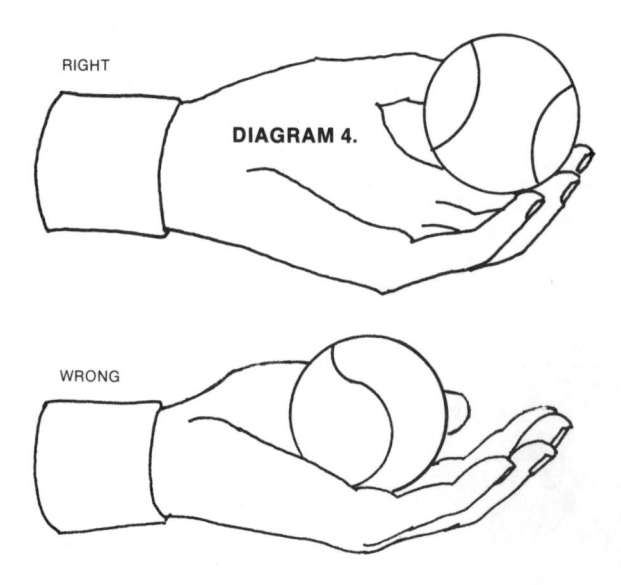

RIGHT

DIAGRAM 4.

WRONG

YOUR FEET SHOULD BE AT AN ANGLE ... to the baseline as you begin your serve. Stand comfortably, with your feet about shoulders' width apart.

SERVICE MOTION. Upon tossing the ball for my serve, I have extended my left arm fully, pointing at the spot where I will make contact.

ball must be tossed with the fingers, not with the hand (Diagram 4). The fingers have more sensitivity, and using them allows you to control the direction of the ball exactly.

Accomplish the toss by a smooth, lifting motion of your arm. With a relaxed wrist movement, release the ball at a point a little above shoulder height. This makes the ball go straight up without any spin. The arm should stay up until the body begins to move forward on the swing.

Look at the ball as you toss it, and keep your eye on it as you serve. That's the only way to get your timing exactly right.

The Swing

Much of the power in serving is obtained from the shift of weight from the front foot to the back foot and back again. The motion of your body, balanced by your arm movements, assures that the full weight of your body will be behind the racket as it smashes into the ball.

While your left arm is moving up for the toss, your right arm, the one holding

20 THE SERVE

THE SERVE (BACK VIEW). (1) As I prepare to serve, my weight is on my front foot. (2) My weight shifts to my back foot as I bring the racket back and begin the toss. (3) I am about to drop my racket arm back and explode forward and

the racket, moves back. Your weight is transferred to your back foot. The racket arm then swings up to meet the ball at the height of the toss. As the racket goes into the ball, your weight shifts forward again, putting power behind the serve. To give you more power, the last part of your swing should be slightly faster than the rest of the swing.

The Point of Contact

During the last part of the swing, the racket naturally snaps upward. Contact is made at the top of the swing, when the arm is fully extended. It is important that you find the most comfortable spot to make contact with the ball and try to toss the ball to that spot on every serve.

The "trigger action" of the wrist is what gives the serve its ultimate control and power (Diagram 5). The wrist should snap just before the moment of contact. All the body movement and swing are just to provide rhythm for this moment of contact.

The Follow-Through

After it has hit the ball, your racket

upward. Notice that I am on my toes, with my whole body poised for the forward weight shift. (4) My weight shifts again onto my front foot, and my back foot remains stationary to help propel me toward the net.

should keep moving. As you can see from Diagram 3, the racket will go down across your body and end up on your left side, pointing to the ground. A smooth follow-through makes your serve a continuous, fluid motion—and that's what gives you power, control, and consistency in your serve.

TYPES OF SERVE

Although every player has his own serving style, there are some basic serves that most players use. Learning

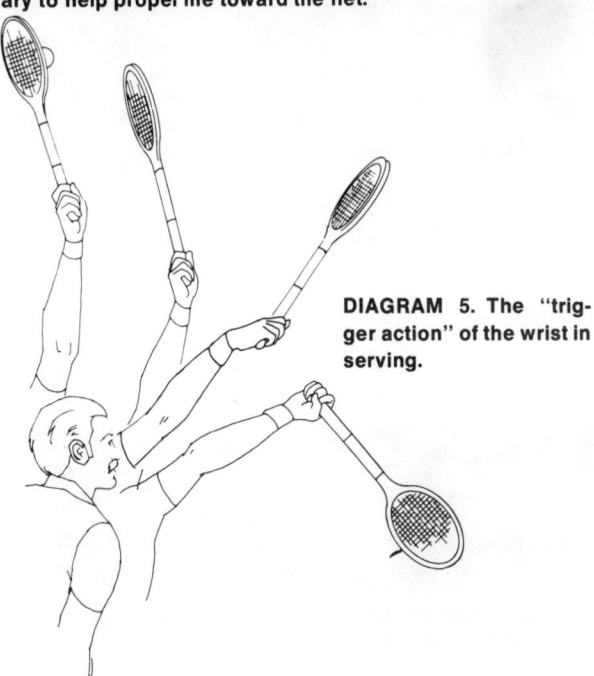

DIAGRAM 5. The "trigger action" of the wrist in serving.

22 THE SERVE

THE SERVE (FRONT VIEW). Arm movements in the serve keep the body balanced. (1) Both my arms move down as I begin the toss. (2) My arms go up in opposite directions as I make the toss and bring the racket back . . .

these serves will help you control any serving situation.

Flat Serve

The flat serve is the simplest tennis serve, the one that's best for beginners. In the flat serve, the racket hits flat against the center of the ball and is at a right angle to the court at the point of contact (Diagram 6). The racket is hit *through* the ball; consequently, the ball will travel in a straight line (Diagram 7). If hit accurately, the flat serve can be very effective. For most beginning and intermediate players, it is the easiest serve to control. Once you've learned to

...(3) As I bring the racket arm back to the back-scratching position, my left arm stays in front for balance. **(4)** On the follow-through, both arms again move down.

place the ball where you want it, you can work on building power.

My best serve is a very fast flat serve. Because I am tall (6 feet, 4 inches), I can hit a hard ball down at a sharp angle, right down my opponent's throat.

Slice Serve

The slice serve is very much like a "slider" in baseball. The ball stays very low after it hits the ground and continues to slide away from the receiver. The slice is fairly easy to learn, and it is very effective as a first serve, especially on fast surfaces.

The main objective of the slice is to pull your opponent off the court, so it is

THE SERVE (SIDE VIEW). Practice over and over until your serve is smooth and consistent. (1) Find the stance that is most comfortable for you. (2) Practice tossing the ball to the same spot every time. (3) Look at

normally used by right-handed players when serving to the forehand court and by left-handed players when serving to the backhand court.

To serve a slice, toss the ball more to the right than usual (if you are serving right-handed). Make the contact at the lower right-hand side of the ball and move your racket upward and around the right side of the ball (Diagram 8).

The slice can be hit with varying degrees of force and *spin*. The greater the angle at which the racket comes around the ball, the more the ball will spin.

American Twist Serve
The American twist, or *overspin,* serve is an advanced shot that requires a lot of power and control. When used by pros such as Roscoe Tanner, it can be deadly. However, it is an easy serve for beginners to serve out of bounds, so if you don't have the twist mastered, it is wiser for you to use the more reliable flat or slice serves.

On this serve, the racket hits upward and sideways into the ball. At the point of contact, the racket head is angled backwards (Diagram 9). As a result, the ball bounces high after it hits and jumps away from the receiver's backhand. Diagram 10 shows the direction the ball travels on a twist serve. As you can see,

the ball as you prepare to hit it. (4) Let your follow-through carry you toward the net.

it is safer to hit this shot to the opponent's backhand court than to his forehand. If you hit to his backhand, he'll have to run almost off the court to return the ball. That leaves the whole court wide open for your next shot.

To serve the twist, toss the ball more to the left than usual (if you are serving right-handed). This means you arch your back and move the racket over to the left on your swing. The racket should move across the ball from left to right. The follow-through is to the right; the racket ends up next to the right leg.

SERVICE STRATEGY

A good server is more than someone who has mastered the basic serves; he is a player who uses his head to outwit his opponent.

I've played in many matches in which my opponent had a good serve and lost because he tried to serve beyond his capabilities on an "off" day. Many players seem to forget that they must play percentage tennis on their serves and not try shots that they merely hope will be successful. Always depend on those shots that you have confidence in and know you can control. Even in championship matches there are more points won on errors than there are on clean placements. Be patient enough to

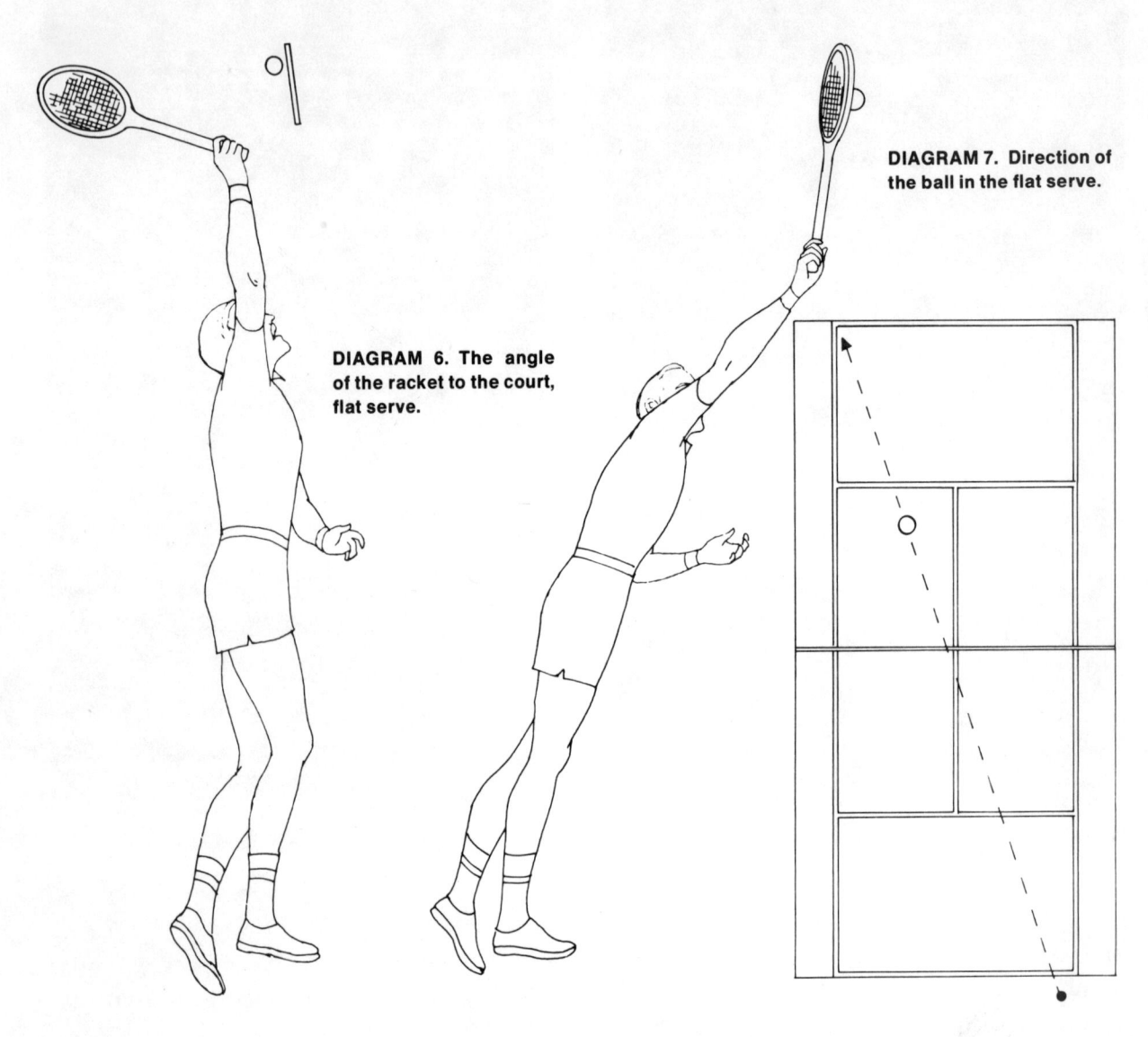

DIAGRAM 6. The angle of the racket to the court, flat serve.

DIAGRAM 7. Direction of the ball in the flat serve.

give your opponent the opportunity to make errors.

If you find yourself missing more serves than usual, stop and think about your normal serve and see if you can get back into the groove. In other words, always try to play *within* your own game and not above it. If you have a particularly good day, be thankful; if you have many good days in a short period, realize that the level of your game has improved and work to keep it at that level. But if you don't perform as well as you might on a particular day, realize what you can expect and play within those limits.

Where to Stand

The rules allow you to stand at any point along the baseline to serve, as long as you are between the center mark and the sideline on the proper side of the court. You might be tempted to move way over toward the alley on your serve because that makes it easier for you to put the ball in your opponent's service court. But remember that you are trying to do

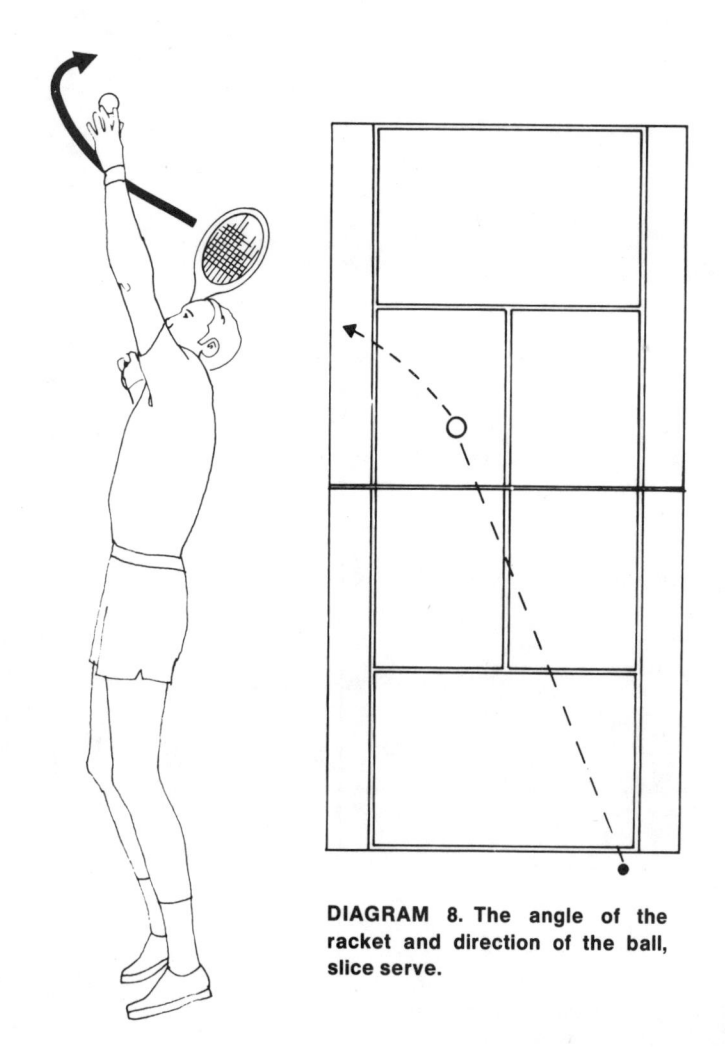

DIAGRAM 8. The angle of the racket and direction of the ball, slice serve.

more than just put the ball in. You must also make the ball difficult for your opponent to return and put yourself in the best possible position to continue play.

On a serve to the forehand court, stand as close to the center line as possible. This will allow you to direct serves to your opponent's backhand and also to cover the court if he returns the ball (Diagram 11).

When you move to the backhand court, you might want to move to the left about 3 feet so that you can hit deep into your opponent's backhand.

Of course, your opponent's game will also determine where you stand. If he's got a wicked backhand, don't serve into it. If he's left-handed, move a little farther away from the center line on the serve to the forehand court.

Placement

In an effective serve, placement is more important than power. Many smaller players—Ken Rosewall, for example—keep their opponents constantly off balance by accurate placement of their serves.

Where you place the ball depends on your strengths and your opponent's weaknesses. For most beginning and intermediate players the backhand is the weaker side, while many advanced players have weaker forehands than

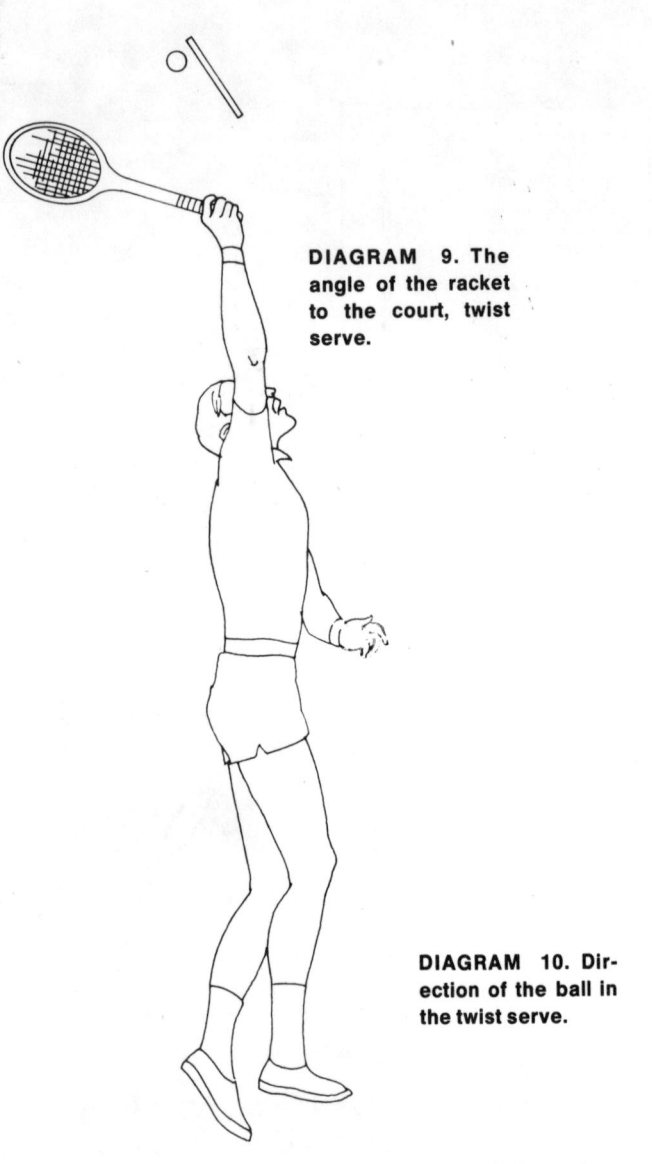

28 THE SERVE

DIAGRAM 9. The angle of the racket to the court, twist serve.

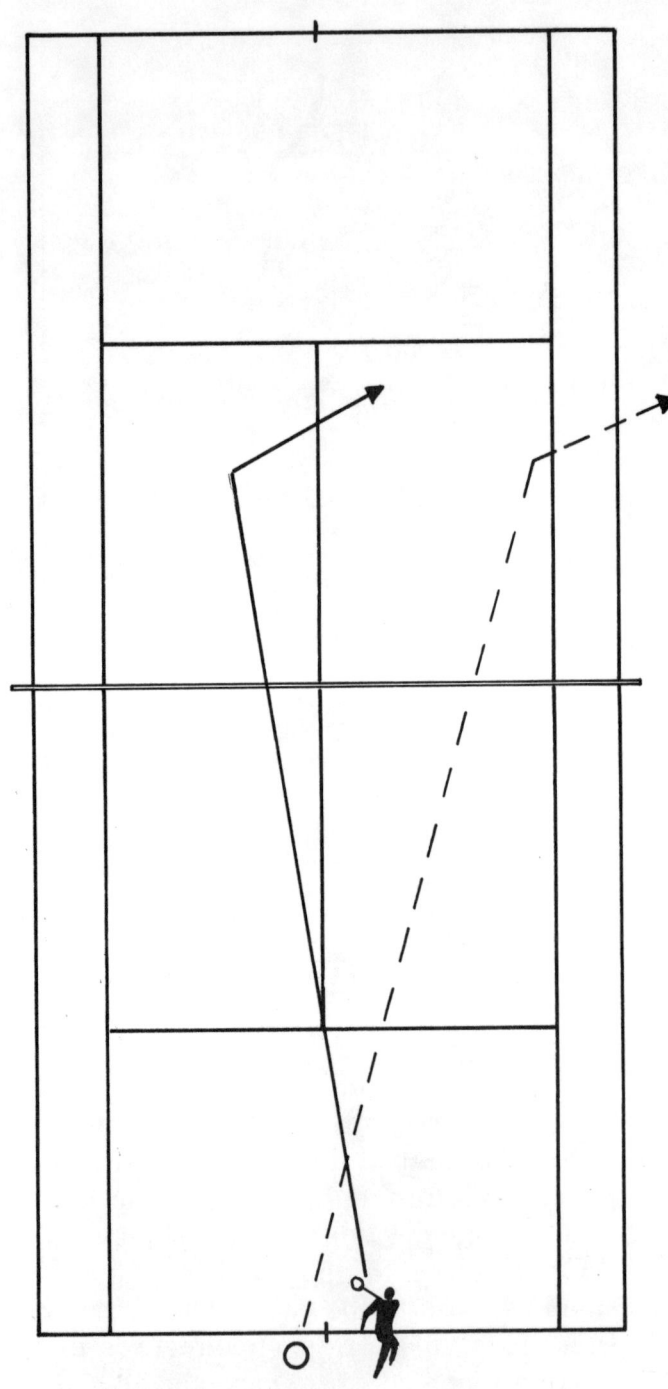

DIAGRAM 10. Direction of the ball in the twist serve.

backhands. As often as possible, place your serve on the other player's weak side.

Mix up your serves so that your opponent can't anticipate your next shot. A very effective serve that most players don't use is the ball hit directly at the receiver so that he is cramped in moving his racket. Another effective serve is the wide shot that makes him run toward the sideline.

First Serve and Second Serve

You get two chances to serve on every point. If you're an average player you probably regard the first serve as a practice shot. So you hit a wild, hard ball, which either goes into the net or sails out of bounds. Then you play it safe on the second serve, hitting a nice, easy predictable shot. After you've done this twice, your opponent knows exactly where you're going to hit. You might as well double fault.

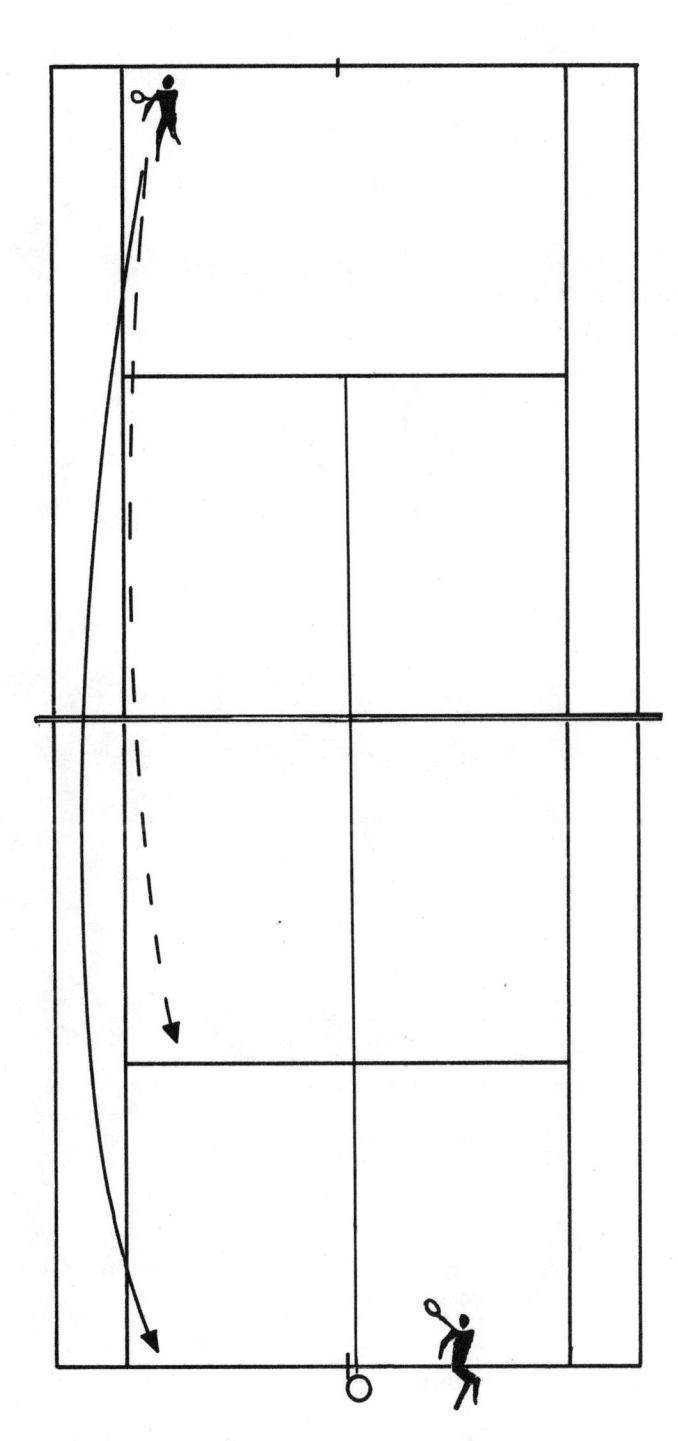

DIAGRAM 11. Here's what can happen if you move too far away from the center line on the serve. Unless you are an exceptionally fast runner, the serve will be returned out of your reach.

Although it's true that you can afford to be somewhat more aggressive on your first serve, you shouldn't try any serve that you haven't mastered in practice sessions. Don't throw this shot away. Your goal is to get your first serve in as often as possible. Only after you begin to get most of your first serves in will you really be in control of your game.

In the 1970 U.S. Open, I lost to Ken Rosewall 6-2, 6-2, 6-2. This wouldn't have happened had I been able to get my first serve in. After that disappointment, I did some hard work on my serve. The result is a matter of public record. I don't think there's any question that my learning to control my serve has been one of the main reasons I've been successful.

Consistency is the key word on the second serve. Most of the pros, including myself, tend to slow down the second serve and put more spin on it. This gives more control over the ball without setting up a perfect shot for the opponent. Control is important on every serve, but on the second serve it's crucial.

It's often been said that the second serve is the real test of a player's serving game. If you know you have a dependable second serve, you'll be more relaxed on your first serve—and being relaxed increases your control and confidence.

GROUNDSTROKES . . . are your basic offensive and defensive weapons and should be practiced until smooth and consistent.

chapter 3
THE BASIC STROKES

After a served ball bounces into the proper service court, the receiver must hit it back over the net. This shot—returning the ball after it has bounced once—is called a *groundstroke*. Groundstrokes are usually hit from the backcourt because of their low angle of bounce. From the backcourt, the player has plenty of room for a good backswing and follow-through. He also has some time to position himself to return the ball in a smooth, rhythmic motion.

If you watch pro tennis on television, you've probably noticed that the pros use far fewer groundstrokes than you do. Instead, they play the *big game*—an aggressive attacking game with lots of *net play*. The basic stroke for net play is the *volley*, a stroke made by hitting the ball before it bounces. I'll talk about volleying and other techniques in a later chapter.

First, however, you must learn to control your groundstrokes. For most tennis players, the groundstroke is the basic offensive and defensive weapon. You'll never be able to hit the more difficult shots that I'll cover later unless you've developed a reliable *forehand* and *backhand*.

THE READY POSITION

Whenever you're not actually hitting or running for the ball you should be in a *ready position*, in the center of the court, either at the baseline or at the net. Assume a comfortable stance, facing the net. Your knees should be slightly bent, and your feet should be about shoulder's width apart. Stand on the balls of your feet, ready to move quickly in either direction.

Hold your racket with its head pointed toward your opponent. Your free hand should support the throat of the racket near its head. In this way you can move the racket quickly either to the forehand or to the backhand.

32 THE BASIC STROKES

THE FOREHAND. (1) As soon as you see that ball is coming toward your forehand, turn your shoulders to the right and bring your racket arm back to this position. (2) At the point of contact, keep your eye on the ball. (3) Make contact when the ball is well in front of your body. (4) As you hit the ball, shift your weight to your front foot. (5) Your follow-through should be in the direction you hit the ball. (6) Although your forehand swing starts low, it should end high above your head.

THE BASIC STROKES 33

THE FOREHAND GRIP

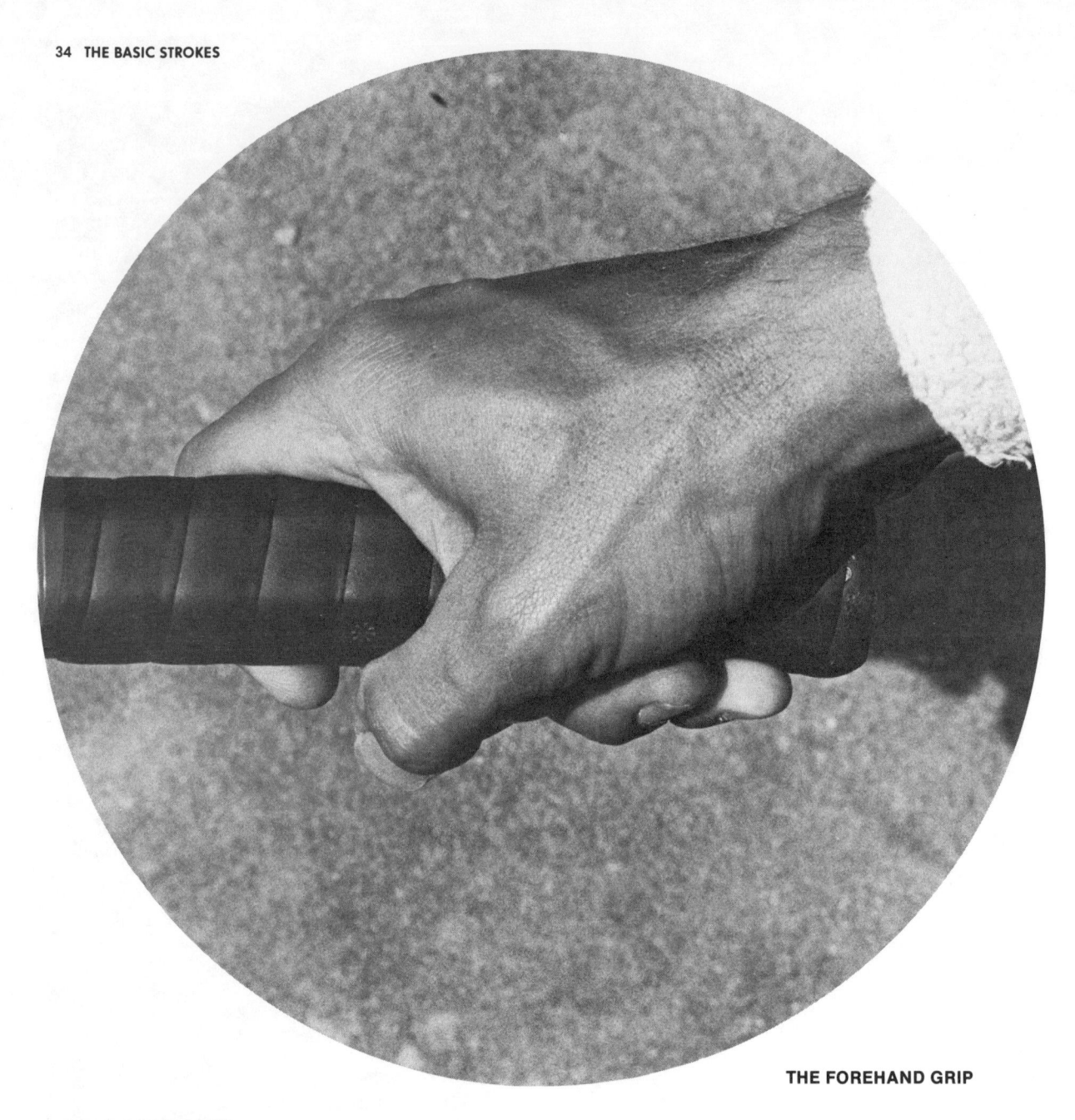

THE FOREHAND

The forehand shot is one that is hit on the same side as your racket arm. In other words, if you are right-handed, your right side is your forehand side. If you are a beginning tennis player, you are probably much more confident about your forehand than about your backhand, because you can use your forehand with greater power.

Grip

As I mentioned in Chapter 2, the Eastern forehand grip is found by "shaking hands" with the racket. Your fingers should be spread slightly apart to prevent a *hammer grip*.

The Stroke

As the ball comes over the net and toward your right side, turn your shoulders to the right, then your hips. Then put your left foot forward so that your body is sideways to the net. While you are running up for the ball, your racket should be back, poised to hit the ball that

THE BACKHAND GRIP

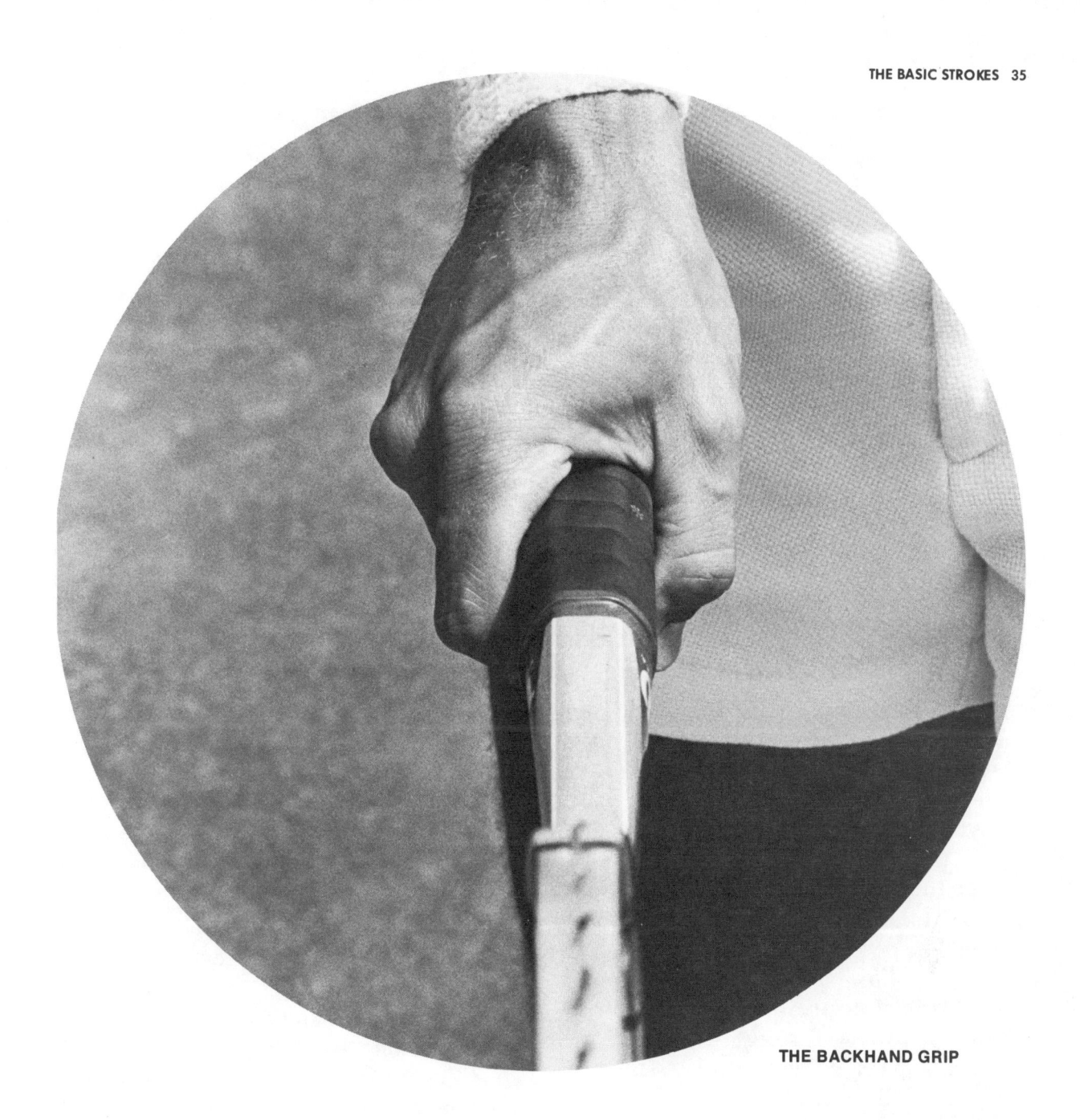

bounces more quickly than you expected.

Bring the racket forward low so that your forward swing will be upward as well as forward, enabling you to put *topspin* on the ball.

Pay special attention to your arm position. You may have problems with your forehand because your arm goes too far away from your body on your backswing. Like the correct golf swing, the correct forehand swing goes from the inside to the outside. This allows you to hit *through* the ball in line with your target. If you find yourself bringing the racket too far back or holding your arm out too straight, take steps to correct the problem. Check to make sure your elbow is next to your body on the backswing. When you swing forward, your elbow will move forward and away from your body.

As in all strokes, the moment of contact is the most important part of the

BEND YOUR KNEES...to get closer to the ground on the half-volley.

shot. As the racket comes forward, your eyes should be focused on the ball. For a well-placed forehand shot, you need a firm yet relaxed wrist that flows forward as you brush the racket through, up, and over the top of the ball. Make contact when the ball is just in front of your front foot. At the point of contact, your racket should be perpendicular to the ground.

Your follow-through should go in the direction you are hitting the ball. A smooth follow-through aimed at the target helps give you control. At the end of the follow-through, your racket should be at the height of your shoulders or head.

THE BACKHAND

The backhand shot is one that is hit on the side of the body opposite the racket arm—in other words, on your left side if you are right-handed. Most top tennis players have better backhands than forehands because they spend hours working on their backhand shots and tend to take their forehand shots for granted.

If you're a beginner, you probably have a weak backhand. You can overcome your fears about hitting a backhand shot if you remember that the backhand is a more natural swing than the forehand—in the backhand, you automatically swing away from your body.

Grip

The backhand grip is the Continental grip you learned to use in serving. If you are right-handed, begin by holding the racket in the forehand position; then turn your hand one-eighth to the left. Spread your fingers for added control. Moving your hand to the left puts more of your hand behind the racket during the backhand motion. Learn to use the backhand grip for all except forehand groundstrokes.

You may have been taught to put your thumb flat against the back of the racket for support. This grip is incorrect. If you fall into this bad habit you will be able to hit the ball in only one spot. If you get caught with the ball behind you, your racket arm just won't be able to get back to the ball.

Flat Backhand

As the ball comes over the net to your left side, turn your shoulders to the left and start bringing your racket back immediately, using your left hand to guide the racket. Your racket should be ready to swing forward when the ball hits the court on your side of the net. You will then be prepared for any bad bounces and will have time to hit the ball while it is still well in front of you.

As you turn your shoulders to the left, your right foot should follow. From this right-foot-forward position, move toward the ball. Time your run so that you end up a few feet from the ball and not right on top of it. As you stop running, your left foot should be your last step so that it breaks your weight movement to the left.

Hold your racket arm in a comfortable position, fairly close but not right up against your body. Bring your arm back at about waist level and swing into the ball by shifting your weight from your left to your right foot. For the flat backhand, the racket face should be perpendicular to the ground at the point of contact. Follow through in the direction you're aiming the ball.

Topspin Backhand

Most of the best tennis players—Laver, Ashe, Okker, and Kodes, for instance—use the *topspin backhand* very effectively. They find that using topspin lets them hit the ball harder, since the spin of the ball brings the ball downward and keeps it in play.

To hit a powerful topspin shot, bring the backswing back lower than you would on a flat backhand shot. Bring the racket forward and upward. The topspin is created by the upward movement of the arm and racket, which brushes over the ball. The follow-through should be at about head height.

Slice Backhand

Because most players use the backhand for defense or for hitting the ball deep into the opponent's court for control, the slice is the most often used backhand shot. The slice keeps the ball in play easily.

The racket arm comes down and forward into the ball, finishing at a little above waist height. The hitting surface is

ON THE SLICE BACKHAND...the hitting surface is at an angle to the ground at point of contact.

38 THE BASIC STROKES

THE BACKHAND STROKE. (1) Prepare early for this shot; as you see the ball coming toward your backhand side, shift your weight to your back foot and turn your shoulders to the left. (2) As you aim at the ball, begin shifting your weight back to the front foot. Never take your eyes off the ball. (3, 4, 5) Meet the ball well in front of your body. Your racket arm should be straight at the point of contact. (6) Your follow-through should be in the direction the ball will travel and (7) end high above your head.

THE BASIC STROKES 39

40 THE BASIC STROKES

DIAGRAM 12. The angle of the racket, slice backhand.

at about a 120-degree angle to the ground at point of contact (Diagram 12).

Two-Handed Backhand

The two-handed backhand has been used effectively by such pros as Jimmy Connors of the United States and Cliff Drysdale of South Africa. Chris and Jeanne Evert have also received wide publicity because they use this shot.

To hit the two-handed backhand, simply bring your left hand down onto the handle of the racket on the backswing. The advantage of the shot, of course, is that it gives you extra power. All of the pros I've just mentioned started playing when they were very young and needed that extra boost. It's a comfortable and easy way for youngsters and other weaker players to hit.

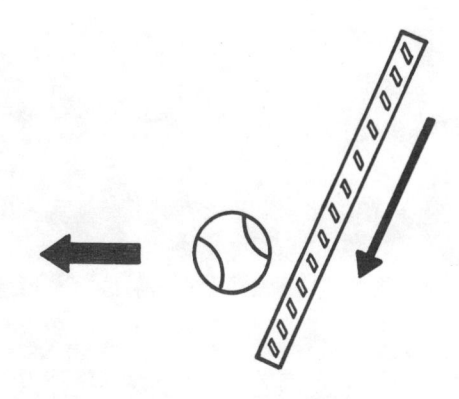

But the two-handed backhand has some limitations of which you should be aware. Because your left hand is on the racket, your reach for wide shots is limited. It's difficult to hit a slice with both hands, and the position is especially awkward for high shots. So, although you may be tempted to use the two-handed approach, make an effort to learn the regular backhand as well—it will increase the scope of your game.

THE SLICE BACKHAND (FACING PAGE).
(1) Prepare early for this shot by bringing the racket arm back and preparing to shift your weight forward. (2) Lean into the ball and meet it well in front of the body. Your racket arm comes down and forward into the ball. Your right shoulder moves into the shot. (3 and 4) On the follow-through, your arms help balance your body as your weight shifts to the front foot.

PLAY PRACTICE GAMES . . . as often as possible to get the feel of competition. You'll soon learn to vary your strokes to adjust to the playing situation.

chapter 4
PLAYING THE GAME

Soon after you move past the instructional stage, you'll realize that it is not enough to have a strong, consistent forehand and backhand, important as these groundstrokes are. The ball very seldom bounces neatly into position, setting you up perfectly for your next shot. On the contrary—the ball goes all over the place, bounces at unexpected angles, and comes at you at all different speeds. To deal with the infinite variety of situations that arise in tennis, you need to develop an arsenal of advanced strokes.

You can practice your simple forehand and backhand shots against a wall or with an instructor who sets up shots for you. You can't master the advanced strokes, however, unless you try them in actual play, when you must move quickly, plan your attack and defense, and hit the ball, all in a matter of seconds. So let's assume you're playing a game—or better yet, that you're watching a movie of yourself playing.

Every once in a while we'll stop the film and analyze what's going on. That way I can show you how to develop strokes that will handle any playing situation.

RETURNING THE SERVE

Your opponent has just served to your forehand service court. Let's slow the film and talk about your movements as you receive the serve.

You should be waiting for the serve in the ready position (see Chapter 3), with your racket out in front of you pointing toward the server. (Although you might feel more comfortable holding the racket in the backhand position across the body, this can cause problems on a fast serve to the forehand.) You should be balanced on the balls of your feet, ready to move quickly in any direction.

Be extra alert and focus on the ball from the moment it is released from the server's hand. By watching carefully, you might be able to tell from the toss or

A GOOD PLAYER...will follow his serve to the net. Here my opponent is moving forward, even before I can return his serve.

swing where your opponent plans to hit the ball. If he throws the ball off to one side, look for a ball that has sidespin. If he throws the ball behind him, his serve will have topspin and may hop in a direction opposite that of the ball's flight. A service toss that is well out in front of the server usually means that you will be returning a flatter, faster serve. It may also mean that the server plans to follow the ball to the net.

As you wait for the serve, hold your left hand at the throat of the racket. If you are watching the ball and keeping alert, you'll have plenty of time to change to either the forehand or the backhand grip. Change the grip by turning the throat of your racket with your left hand. Hold the racket with either the forehand or backhand grip, whichever is your weaker shot. It will probably be easier to change to the grip of your stronger stroke as you see the ball come over the net.

As the ball comes over the net, bring the racket back quickly by turning your shoulders. Take a short backswing. Especially on a hard, straight serve, your return may be little more than a block. The speed of the serve will return the ball.

As you hit the ball, your weight shifts forward. You should still be on the balls of your feet, moving to return the next shot.

FOLLOWING THE SERVE TO THE NET

Now let's back up the film and watch your opponent's movements after he serves the ball. If he is just an average

A WELL-PLACED APPROACH SHOT...keeps the receiver back at the baseline so that the hitter can control the net.

player, one who relies mainly on his groundstrokes, he probably is still back at the baseline and has moved into the ready position for your return.

But if he's a better, more aggressive player (and we'll assume he is), he might let the momentum of his weight shift and follow-through carry him toward the net, where he'll be ready to return your next shot with a volley.

This is the kind of play you're seeing more and more of in professional and advanced tennis. Going to the net after the serve is an attacking move, one that demands quick thinking, agility, and speed. Let's stop and talk about how you can incorporate this offensive maneuver into your game.

One of the most important elements in *rushing the net* is speed. If you hit a hard, fast serve, you have much less time to get up to the net than if you hit a slower slice serve. If you can also put some topspin on the ball to weaken your opponent's return, so much the better.

If you intend to rush the net, toss the serve farther in front than you normally would. You will then be carried forward by the momentum of your follow-through. Although you may not be able to get all the way to the net before your opponent returns the ball, you should get close enough to return his shot with a deep volley that keeps him behind the baseline hitting a defensive shot.

Timing is another crucial element in this maneuver. If your opponent's reactions are faster than yours, you won't be able to move up very far before the ball comes back to you. You've got to start

PLAY WITHIN YOUR GAME... and don't attempt shots you can't play. Remember, even in championship matches there are more points won on errors than there are on clean placements.

moving immediately after the point of contact on your serve. You can't wait to see if your serve was good before you start moving. Obviously, rushing the net is not the best move for a player who is slow or who has an unreliable serve, or who is playing against someone with a particularly good return of serve. If you're such a player, you'd better remain in the backcourt where you can control your shots or wait for the right opportunity to attack.

APPROACH SHOTS

Let's assume that both you and your

PLAYING THE GAME 47

THE FOREHAND APPROACH SHOT ... should be hit deep into the opponent's court, usually to his backhand, if this is his weakest stroke. (1) Keep your **body low** and let your momentum give you power as you move toward the net. Make contact with the ball well in front of your body. (2) Keep moving quickly toward the net as you follow through. Control and placement are more important than how hard you hit.

opponent are fairly advanced players. He is moving toward the net after his serve, and he hits a *short shot*, a shot that lands between the net and your service line. You now have a chance to hit an *approach shot*. With an approach shot, you try to force your opponent to stay behind the baseline and keep him on the defensive (Diagram 13). This shot is used most often on clay and other slow surfaces.

Forehand

To hit a forehand approach shot, take

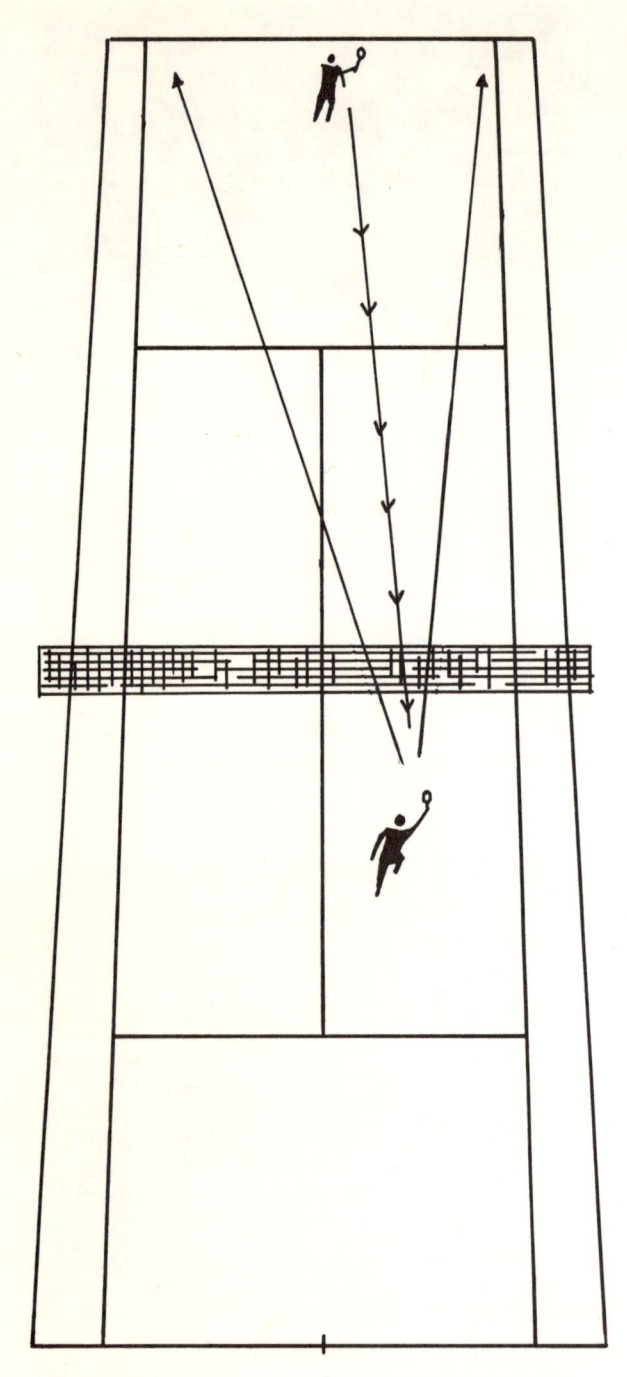

DIAGRAM 13. Angle and placement of approach shots.

only a short backswing, bending to hit the ball. Your follow-through should be at least shoulder high. This will put topspin on the ball and keep it in the court. After hitting the shot, continue forward to a position where you can cover any possible *passing shots*.

Backhand

The backhand approach shot is especially important for the net rusher. Hit this shot just as you would the forehand approach shot—as *deep* (close to the baseline) into the opponent's court as possible. You don't have to hit the ball hard. If you hit it deep, you will have more time to get to the net, and your opponent will find his passing shot more difficult to hit.

A backhand approach shot is usually hit with a slice. The ball will then stay low, making the passing shot more difficult.

PASSING SHOTS

Now let's look at the actions of your opponent. Your approach shot has put him on the defensive, keeping him on or behind the baseline. You are now at the net.

His objective will be to hit a passing shot, one that goes past you at the net and into your side of the court. Obviously, he must hit a shot that is out of the reach of your racket (Diagram 14). This will usually mean a *down the line* shot; a *crosscourt* shot would travel across your body, making it easy for you to return the ball. A *lob*, which goes over your head, can also be considered a passing shot.

An effective passing shot goes past the net player and all the way to the baseline. Unless you're really speedy, you won't be able to get to the ball in time and he'll score a point.

PLAYING THE NET

The "film" we've just watched makes one point clear: in advanced tennis, the player who controls the net and the forecourt controls the game. The strong net player can put his opponent on the defensive right from the beginning and,

THE BACKHAND APPROACH SHOT . . . is usually hit with a slice. (Above) Keep your knees bent and your body low as you shift your weight into the ball. (Below) Keep running toward the net as you follow through for control. The ball should go deep into your opponent's backcourt.

50 PLAYING THE GAME

THE VOLLEY. (1) In the ready position, stand with your racket pointing toward your opponent, with the throat of the racket in your left hand (if you are right-handed). Stand on the balls of your feet and keep your knees bent. (2 and 3) On both the ...

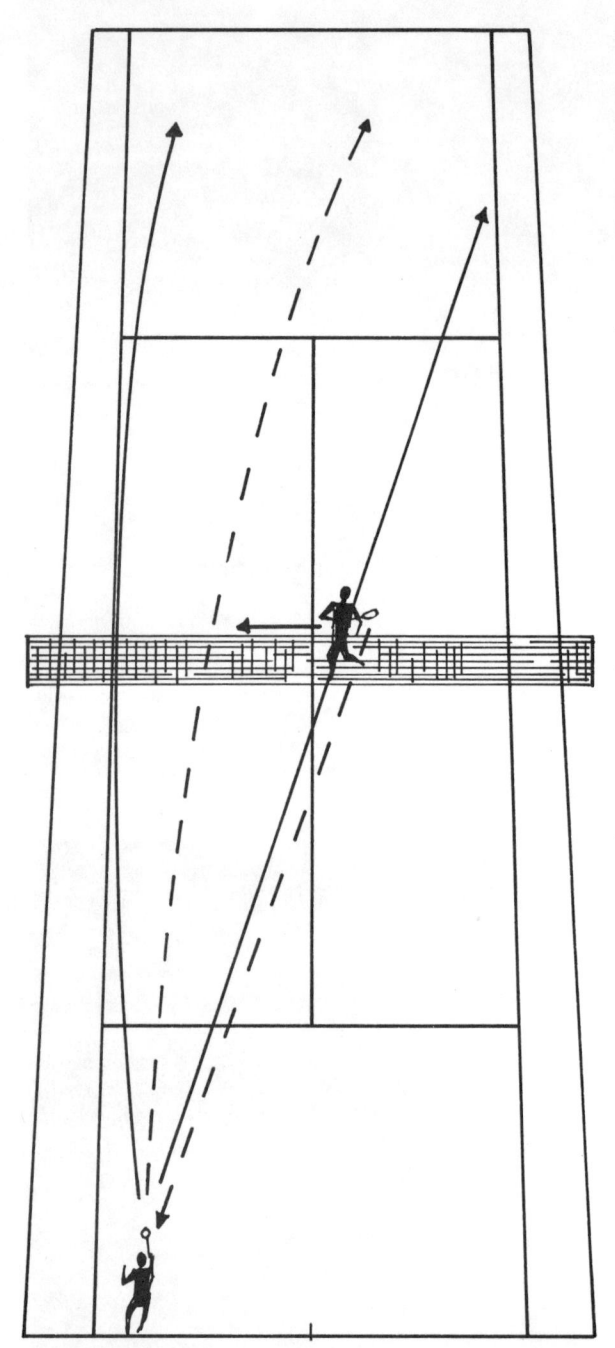

DIAGRAM 14. A passing shot hit down the line, past the player at the net.

with clever strategy, can keep him scrambling for the ball. To master net play, you must know how to use the *volley*, the *half-volley*, the *drop shot*, the *lob*, and the *overhead shot* or *smash*.

THE VOLLEY

A volley is a ball that is hit before it

PLAYING THE GAME 51

... forehand and the backhand volleys, make a short backswing by turning your shoulders, your hips, and then your feet. Prepare to step forward as the racket comes toward the ball. (4) Make contact with the ball when it is well in front of the body. (5) Step forward as you move into the ball. (6) Use your other arm to help keep your movements smooth and balanced.

52 PLAYING THE GAME

THE HALF-VOLLEY... is hit immediately after the ball has bounced. Pick up the ball with your racket much as an infielder in baseball would pick up a ball that bounced just in front of his glove. Keep the ball as low as possible.

bounces. The stroke is hit with a sharp, punching motion rather than with a swing. Most players take a full swing for the volley, but a short punch is faster and easier to control and gives your opponent less time to react.

Grip

On groundstrokes, you have time to change grips as the ball comes over the net. You don't have that time when you're at the net. Because you need more strength for the backhand than for the forehand, use your backhand grip for volleying.

Hold your racket in the ready position. As you approach the net, watch the ball very closely; the closer you are to the net, the less time you'll have to react.

Forehand

If the ball comes to your right side, turn your shoulders immediately to the right. This automatically turns the racket so that it points to the right. That's all the backswing you need. Shift your weight forward as you step with the left foot.

Backhand

If the volley comes to your left side, turn

THE POINT OF CONTACT...is the most important part of the backhand shot (and of all other shots as well).

A SHORT, SHARP PUNCH...with no follow-through is the most effective stroke on the volley.

AN OFFENSIVE LOB ... can be used in the same situations as you would hit a passing shot. I'm hitting this lob from right inside the baseline, high and deep into my opponent's backhand.

your shoulders to the left. The left hand stays on the racket while it comes back with the turn of the shoulders. Step forward with your right foot as you make contact with the ball. Your stroke should be a short jab or punch.

THE HALF-VOLLEY

A half-volley is a shot that is hit immediately after the bounce. Usually it is better for you to run up to the ball and volley it or run back and let it bounce all the way up before hitting it, but occasionally you can use the half-volley to catch your opponent off guard.

Hit the half-volley as you would a groundstroke, but bend your knees more to get closer to the ground. Use less backswing than you would on a groundstroke.

DROP SHOTS

A drop shot is a ball that is hit just barely over the net. Most of the drop shots you hit will be volleys. To hit a drop shot, use your volley stroke, but slow the ball down by putting plenty of underspin on

THE DEFENSIVE LOB . . . can be used to change the pace of a game and give you time to get back in position. Lob high and deep so you'll have time to get back to the middle of the court.

it. The ideal drop shot will hardly bounce at all. A well-placed drop shot is devastating when your opponent is back at the baseline. But if he's closer in and you hit it so it bounces too high, you're giving him the perfect setup for a lob or a passing shot.

THE LOB

A lob is a high passing shot hit over the opponent's head. With the emphasis on net play in modern tennis, the lob is becoming an offensive as well as a defensive weapon. You can use an offensive lob in the same situations in which you use a passing shot. Hit the ball just high enough to clear your opponent's outstretched racket. Make sure your feet are set in position because you are trying to force your opponent with this shot.

The offensive lob is usually hit with topspin, but if you catch your opponent off balance or when he is lunging toward the net, topspin is not necessary. If you're not using topspin, conceal your intentions. In other words, try to approach the shot as if you were going to hit a flat or *underspin* passing shot and

DIAGRAM 15. The overhead, or smash.

hold the backswing as long as possible in order to make your opponent commit himself before you do. Hit the ball as deep as possible into your opponent's backhand corner.

The topspin offensive lob is usually hit with the forehand. The racket should be brought back low and brought forward and up abruptly with the wrist.

Since the swing and contact must be perfectly timed, I don't recommend that beginning and intermediate players attempt this shot very often.

Instead, use the lob defensively. If your opponent hits an approach shot that puts you in a weak position to return a passing shot, hit a lob instead. If you lob the ball high and deep, you'll have time to scramble toward the middle of the court. You'll then be back on even terms instead of being in an almost hopeless position.

THE SMASH

The overhead shot, or smash, is an aggressive shot used to return a lob. The smash is hit hard and straight down. For most players, that means it goes right into the net. If you study the movements in the accompanying photo sequence and in Diagram 15, you can turn your overhead into a deadly offensive weapon. Otherwise, your opponent will feed you a lot of lobs, knowing you can't return them.

The grip used on the smash is the Continental grip, the same grip used for the serve. The last part of the serve is the arm motion that is used for the overhead. The backswing is shorter for the smash, however. I like to think of the motion of the smash as hammering a nail into the wall.

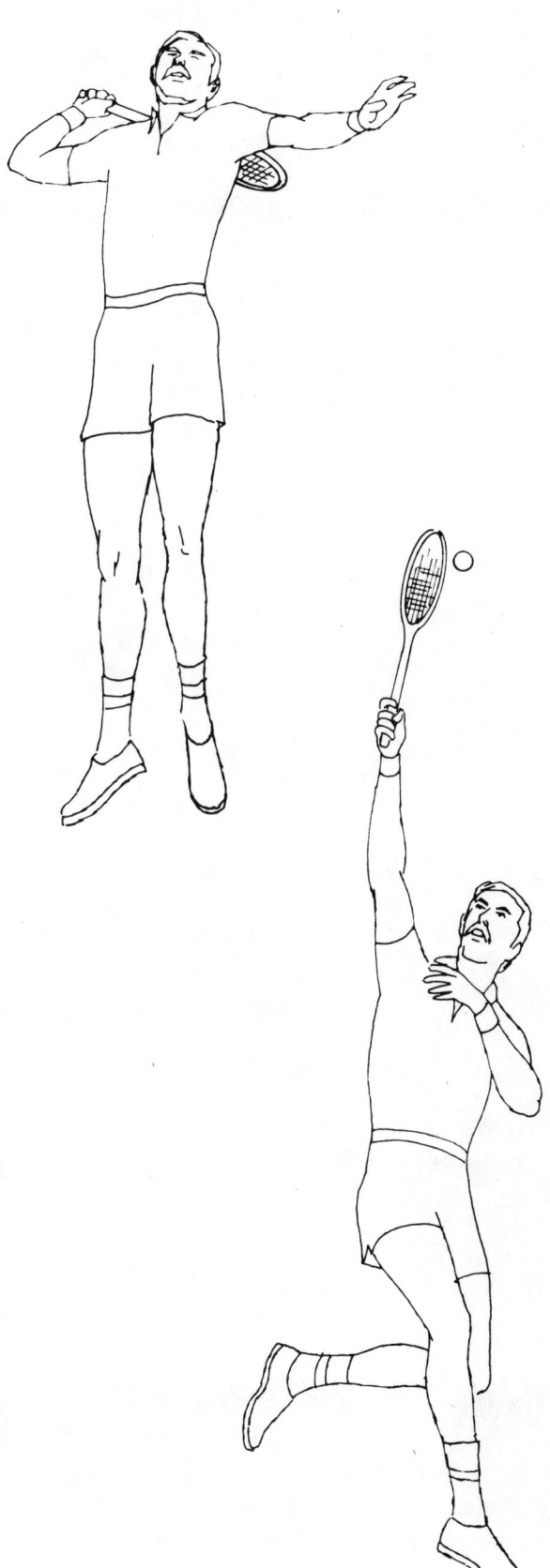

When you see that your opponent is going to lob, immediately bring your racket behind your head. Make sure you move back far enough so that you can step into the ball. If the ball starts to get behind you, jump off the right foot to reach for it.

If you don't have time to get into position before the ball bounces or if the lob is very high, move back and hit your smash on the bounce. It is better to allow your opponent more time to get into position than it is to hit the ball when you are off balance.

58 PLAYING THE GAME

THE SMASH. (1) Keep your eye on the ball as you begin moving your racket arm back into the back-scratching position. (2) Use your left hand to line up the ball and to balance the action of the racket arm. Your left hand can also shade your eyes in bright sunlight. (3) Complete the smash as you would the serve, allowing your shifting body weight to lend its power to your shot.

Hit the overhead flat, with very little spin, and follow-through as you would on the serve. Your arm should be fully extended at the point of contact. The best smash is one hit very deep into a corner or away from your opponent. As with the serve, placement and angle are more important than speed.

With this arsenal of strokes and with some basic understanding of strategy, you're well on your way to becoming an effective tennis player. As often as possible, play actual games in addition to practicing. You'll soon find you can handle various tennis situations with ease.

TENNIS ACTION IS FAST ... so you must learn to anticipate your opponent's shots. Familiarity with the principles of tennis strategy will help you play a consistently better game.

chapter 5
WINNING TACTICS

Although you should practice as much as possible to develop a consistent, strong serve, a solid forehand and backhand, and competent strokes, you won't be able to play winning tennis without one vital quality: *intelligence*. I can't stress this point enough. The player who wins is the one who can think on his feet.

But you won't be able to think quickly unless you've acquired some basic understanding of tactics, and that's why I've written this chapter. Some of my points will probably seem self-evident, but it's surprising how few players really pay attention to them—if they did, they'd play better tennis.

ANALYZE YOUR OWN GAME

You probably know at least one player (you may be one yourself) who invariably tries to smash his first serve down his opponent's throat, only to have the ball end up in the net or out of bounds. He does this on every serve, never having the brains to admit that he just can't control the ball when he hits it that hard. So he continues to double fault or to hit easy second serves that his opponent creams. That's the classic example of someone who doesn't analyze his own game.

Another player serves well but just stands there at the baseline watching to see whether his serve was good. Time and again he finds himself moving toward the net too late to hit his opponent's short or high return.

Those are the most obvious examples, but every player has some weaknesses of which he is not aware. Whatever your weakness is, you can be sure your opponent will discover it if you don't. If you can't isolate what's wrong yourself, have your instructor or a better player watch you play.

Sometimes some aspect of your game will remain weak even though you practice to correct it. If you're a weekend

USE YOUR LEFT HAND...to guide the racket on the backswing of your backhand shots.

tennis player, for example, you probably lack the speed of someone who plays more regularly. Try to place your shots so that your opponent will have to return them to the center of the court. Then place your shots to keep him running all over the place until he's so worn out that he has no more speed than you do. We've all seen older players beat younger ones by using just this tactic. That's playing smart tennis.

Know your own strengths as well as your weaknesses. Most average players have strong forehands and weaker backhands. If that's your case, you naturally want to play so that the other player hits to your forehand most of the time. If he's an average player, one way to do this is to hit to his backhand. Since the backhand crosses the body, the most natural direction for the ball to go is straight to your forehand. Or, set a trap for him by moving over a little to your left, leaving your forehand court open. Chances are he'll hit the ball right into that open space, exactly where you want him to.

ANALYZE YOUR OPPONENT

Your opponent's strengths and weaknesses will determine how you use yours. If his backhand is strong, don't play to it. If his forehand is strong, hit to his backhand.

Every opponent has a different personality, so you have to vary your strategy for each one. Some players try 100 percent on every point, while others will pace themselves for the crucial points later in the match. If your opponent is a pusher, try to wear him out; if he's a pacer, make double sure you're conserving your own strength as well. Some players play well when they're leading but fold if you get ahead and keep the pressure on. Others have a "never say die" attitude, and you must be careful not to relax your lead.

Most players feel more comfortable receiving slower shots. However, your opponent may be one of those exceptional players who prefer to play against a hard-hit ball, using the force of their opponent's shots to increase their own pace. Try to slow down your game or use more spins against such a player. It is often said that you should try to keep the other player away from the net. However, some players like to rush the net behind a well-planned approach shot but are uncomfortable with unexpected drop shots. Some players move well laterally but can't move backward or forward.

Once you've analyzed your opponent, you can force him to play the style of game that is most to your liking. It is wise to adjust your game for your opponent, but don't let him dictate the style of play. Let your strengths combined with your opponent's weaknesses win for you.

ANTICIPATING

A smart player learns to judge where his opponent is going to hit the ball. If you've played against someone often, you've already learned his pattern of play. Perhaps he always returns a shot to his backhand court with a down-the line passing shot. If you know that's his pattern, move immediately to your left after you hit your shot.

Even if your opponent's playing patterns are unfamiliar to you, you can position yourself fairly well just by studying the angles of return. Let's say your opponent is standing in the backcourt and you are in your forecourt near the sideline. You hit a shot down the line into his backhand court (Diagram 16). Since he has to run over to his left to return the ball, he won't have time to place a shot into your backhand. Even if he hits toward the backhand corner, the area you have to cover in the forecourt is relatively small. All you have to do is move to your left after you hit the ball, and you'll be safe.

If you were to hit the same shot to his forehand, the possible area of return would be much larger. You'd have to move much farther to your left to cover the return.

A good general rule is to try to get into the center of the possible return area. That way both your forehand and your backhand can be put to use.

Because tennis is a game of fast action, you have to keep in constant motion in order to be in the right place. Timing is important here, too: you have to run a lot faster if you're volleying than if you're hitting rallies from the backcourt.

Finally, anticipation involves *watching the ball* and *watching your opponent*. The direction his shoulders turn will tell you if he plans to hit forehand or backhand. His feet will show you where he plans to run. He'll signal

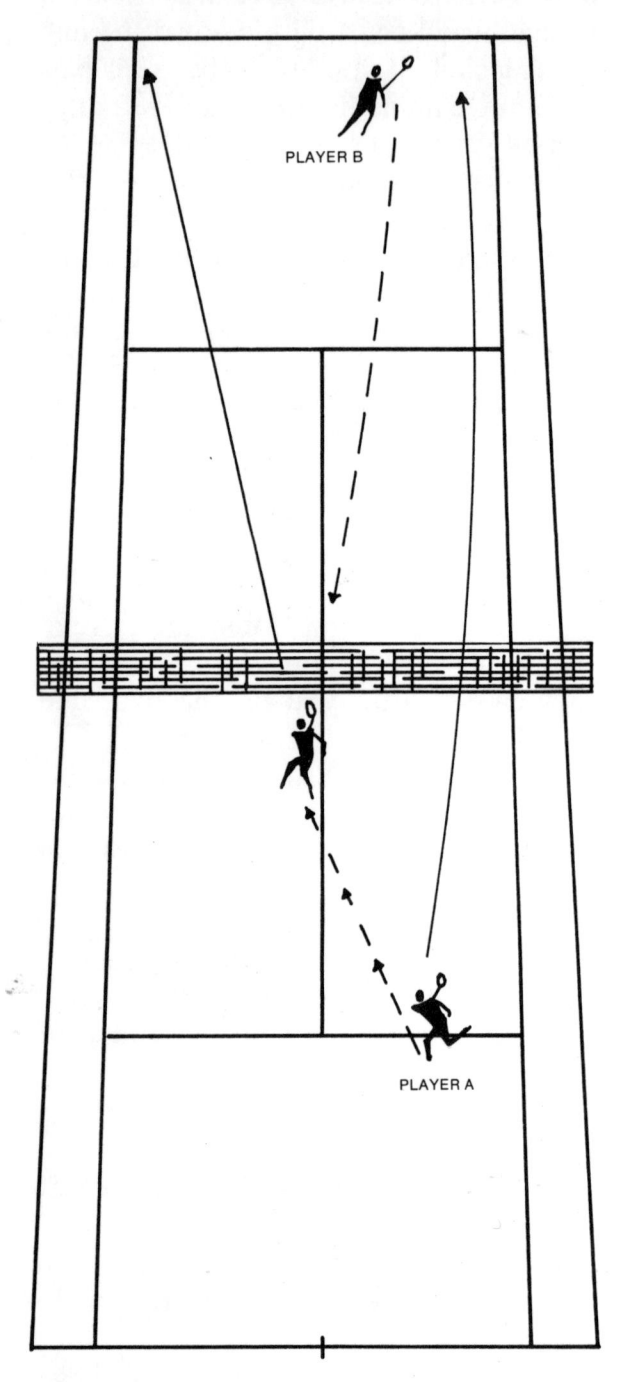

DIAGRAM 16. Possible angles of return in a typical tennis exchange.

that he's going to lob by bringing his racket down low—that's your cue to start moving back. If you consciously notice the *trajectory* of the ball, you'll be better able to place it right where you want it.

VARIETY

In Chapter 4, I showed you some of the shots that add variety to your game. Smart players keep their opponents guessing by using their full repertoire of strokes.

Here's another place where you learn the value of knowing your own game. If you always return an approach shot to the forehand with a passing shot to the backhand, your opponent has probably noticed it and moved toward the backhand. That's the time to change your pattern and hit into his forehand. Be aware of your own playing patterns and change them often enough to keep your opponent off guard.

Change the rhythm of your play, too. Follow a series of hard, flat shots with a slow slice. Your opponent has come to expect a certain speed in your responses —don't live up to his expectations. Even if he's murdering you with fast balls, you can slow the pace by feeding him nice, gentle lobs until he's too frustrated to play well.

RELAX AND CONCENTRATE

Both of these seemingly contradictory qualities are vital for playing good competitive tennis. Relaxation is important for several reasons. If you are relaxed you will not tire as quickly or be as susceptible to cramps in a long, close match. Your timing and rhythm will be better. You will probably move faster on the court and enjoy your game more.

Good concentration is the factor that

NET PLAY...demands quick thinking, agility, and speed.

separates the champions from the "almost" champions. You must be able to relax, think, and perform better than your opponent in tight situations. If you feel you are getting tense, stop and take a deep breath and focus your mind on the strategy of your next point. It also helps to let your body go limp as you are changing courts. Make a conscious effort to slow down your racing nerves.

ADJUSTING TO PLAYING CONDITIONS

Recently indoor courts have made tennis a year-round, all-weather sport. But most of us still play on outdoor courts, and we have to make allowances for court conditions, sun, wind, and weather.

Court Surfaces

Although you don't change your basic game, you must vary your game on different playing surfaces because the bounce of the ball is different on clay, grass, cement, and synthetic surfaces.

On grass a fast-moving ball will slide away and stay low after it hits. Most grass courts are in poor condition, so you get many irregular and unexpected bounces. When the pros play on grass, they serve, rush to the net, and try not to

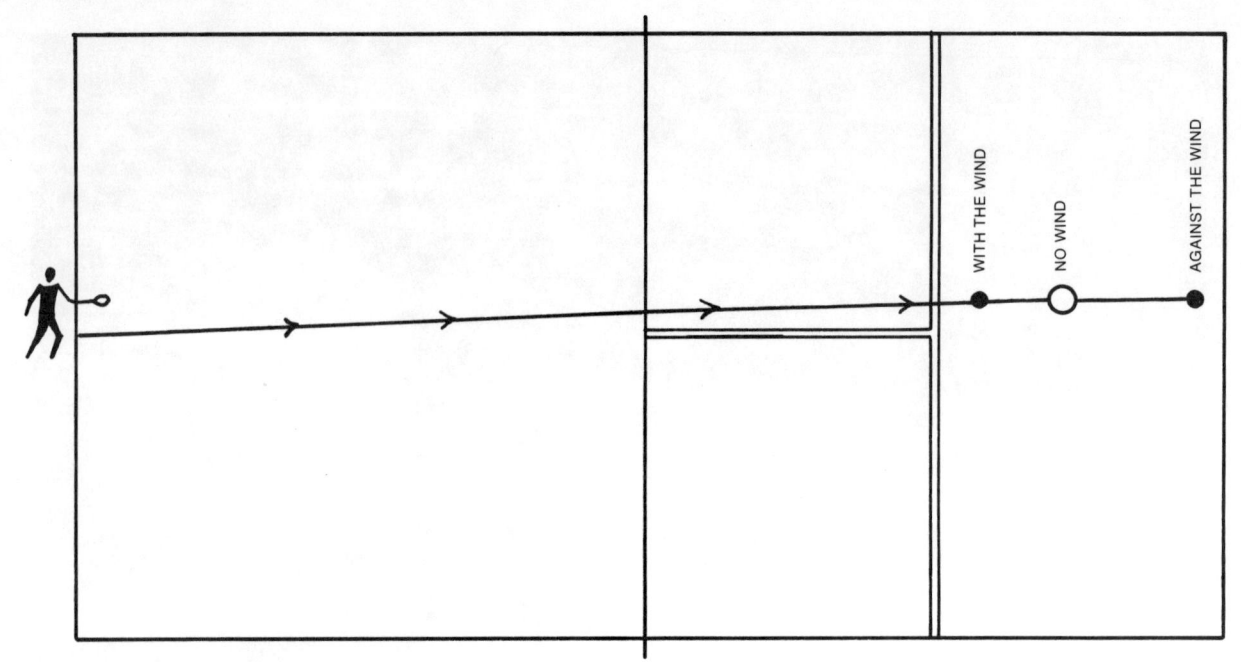

DIAGRAM 17. Adjusting for the wind.

let the return of serve bounce. Matches on grass are characterized by fast points and bad bounces.

On cement a ball will almost always bounce true, but the speed of the court varies greatly. Play aggressively on fast cement; stay in the backcourt on slow cement.

Clay is the slowest of the surfaces—when the ball hits it grabs more than on smoother courts. A careful, less aggressive strategy should be used. There is usually a greater variety of shots on clay. Players must learn to slide into their shots because the top layer of the court is loose. Use more drop shots and change of pace and use patience in picking the right spot for your attack.

The synthetic surfaces usually have a uniform bounce, but they vary so much in speed that I can't recommend any one strategy. In general, the faster the surface, the more forceful your game should be.

Wind

Playing in the wind can be very frustrating. The most important thing is to have the proper mental preparation, because playing in the wind presents an extra factor in your strategy. You must realize that the wind presents equal problems for your opponent, and if you are better than he is at coping with the wind, you will have a real advantage. Diagram 17 shows where to place your shots to adjust for wind.

When the wind is blowing at your back, temper your shots a little and take the net, especially on a fast surface. Aim your shots shorter and keep your opponent running—remember, he's *against* the wind.

If you are the one hitting against the wind, hit your shots harder and deeper. The lob can be especially effective because the ball will move erratically in the air. It will be difficult for your opponent to hit a smash without sailing it out of bounds. When you are serving in the wind, toss the ball a little lower than usual.

Sun and Lights

Particularly at midday, the sun will

cause problems on your serve and smash. Try changing the spot where you serve, changing your stance, or changing your toss. By trial and error, you can find the place where the light is least distracting. Of course it helps if you can do this experimenting before the actual match, but that's not always possible.

On overhead shots you can sometimes block the light by extending your left hand upwards. Use the sun and lights to your advantage by lobbing more than usual.

Heat and Humidity

High temperatures and humidity can have a great effect on your tennis game, but there are ways you can minimize the negative effects. If you are a social player, plan to play in the cooler parts of the day, and do not overexert yourself, particularly if you're overweight.

If you're playing in a tournament, you don't have the luxury of picking the time for your match, and you must be prepared for the most extreme conditions. It is often helpful to take salt tablets or extra table salt before playing. Drink some liquid when changing sides, but don't bloat yourself. Other suggestions: Wear a hat and wristbands to keep sweat from running down onto your racket hand. Use sawdust to keep your hands dry.

Make a conscious effort to relax and slow down your movements. Think cool —remember, it's just as hot for the other player as it is for you.

DOUBLES ... is the form of tennis most weekend players enjoy. In doubles, you have to learn to think and act as a team rather than as individuals.

chapter 6
DOUBLES

For many players and spectators, doubles play is more enjoyable than singles. Playing doubles brings teamwork into tennis. There is great satisfaction in working effectively with your teammate in a competitive situation. Doubles also has a social side—*mixed doubles* (in which each team has one man and one woman player) is probably the form of tennis with which weekend players are most familiar. Playing doubles is ideal for the player who is out of shape or who doesn't want to put forth the energy that singles tennis demands.

From the standpoint of the spectator, championship doubles is sometimes a much more exciting game than singles. Tournament doubles feature teamwork, fast shots, and power plays mixed with delicate touch shots. Spectators also enjoy the contrasting styles and strategies of different teams.

It is not always true that the best singles players make the best doubles players. The most important factor in doubles is the interaction of the two players on a team, who must play together rather than as individuals. Bob Lutz and I started playing doubles together when we were juniors, and we were able to achieve many victories in men's doubles play before we were able to make an impact in singles competition. Our success was due to our familiarity with each other's tactics and our ability to anticipate each other's moves.

RULES FOR DOUBLES

The basic rules for playing and scoring doubles are the same ones used for singles. However, there are some rules that apply specifically to doubles play, and you should be aware of them before you begin.

Court Dimensions

The doubles court is 9 feet wider than the singles court (see Diagram 1,

THE BEST DOUBLES PARTNER...is one whose style of play exactly complements your own. Eric van Dillen and I were the Number One doubles team in 1972 and 1973.

Chapter 1). The ball may land in the area called the *alley* on any doubles shot except the serve without being out of bounds. The area into which you must serve, however, remains the same as in singles tennis.

Serving Order

At the beginning of each set, you and your partner will decide who will serve first. The serve then alternates with each game. In a foursome, this means that Player A will serve game 1, 5, 9, 13, and so on until the end of the set. Player A's partner, Player B, would serve games 3, 7, 11, and so on. The order of serve may be changed at the end of the set.

Both teams must decide their order of service before the set begins, and that order must be kept throughout the set. If a player serves in the wrong order, any points won or lost during his service are discounted. Play then resumes in the proper order.

Receiving Order

Before a set begins, the partners on each team decide from which side of the court each of them will receive the serve. Once he has chosen either the forehand or backhand court, a player will continue to receive the serve in that court throughout the match. If the partners decide they would like to switch sides, they may do so at the end of a set.

PLAYING THE GAME

Although you use the same basic strokes in doubles as you do in singles, you must make some changes in your playing style because you now have a partner. In general, doubles requires less running and thus less endurance than singles, but in doubles it is even more important to control the ball and place it carefully.

Serving

To serve in doubles, stand a bit farther from the center line than you do in singles—in fact, you can move to halfway between the center line and sideline. This gives you a better chance of serving into your opponent's backhand. Since you have a partner to cover the other side of the court, the ball won't be returned out of reach as it would on a singles serve.

It is usually best in doubles to use a slice or American twist serve instead of attempting a cannonball. This will give you more time to move toward the net, where you can more easily dominate the game. Another advantage is that these serves don't travel in a straight line, so that gives you a better chance of opening up some holes in the other team's defense. If you can get both players to move toward their backhand court by hitting a twist serve, your net man can hit a drop shot or deep volley to their forehand side.

Immediately after you serve, move up toward the net and prepare to begin volleying. Or, if your partner moves across to poach the ball, move quickly to cover the area he has left unprotected (Diagram 18).

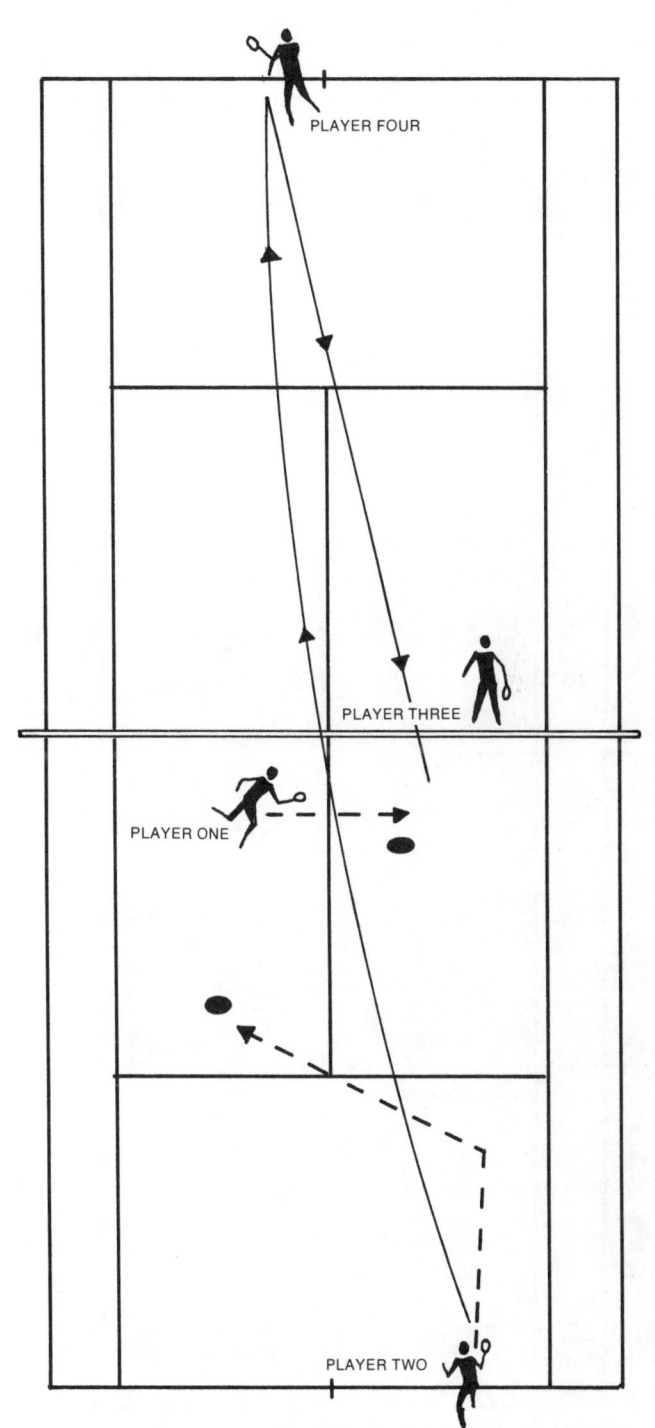

DIAGRAM 18. Covering the area left vacant when your partner is poaching.

72 DOUBLES

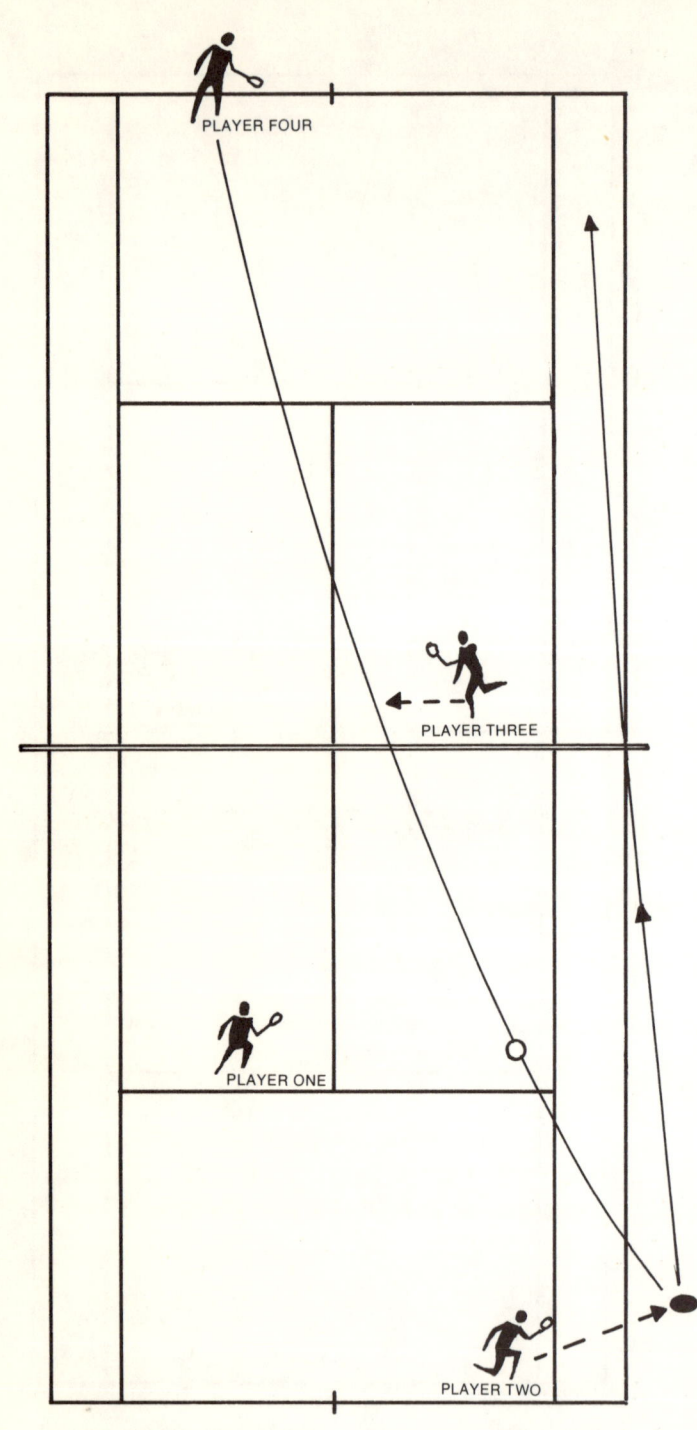

DIAGRAM 19. Returning the serve when the opposing net man is poaching.

Returning the Serve

In singles, the serve may be returned safely anywhere in the singles court. In doubles, however, your return must be more precise because one of your opponents is at the net blocking off half of the court. If your return is hit to the net, or if it "floats" to the other side, a good net man will probably end the point.

Most service returns should be hit directly back to the server, who is probably rushing the net. Keep the ball low so that he is forced to hit up. There's a good chance he'll set up your partner at the net. If the opposing net man is poaching, hit down his alley behind him (Diagram 19).

If you are having trouble returning the service, try a number of lobs, but be sure to let your partner know so he will move back and be ready if you hit a shallow lob. Lobbing serves to break up the rhythm of the other team, especially if they are both strong net men.

Controlling the Net

The basic objective in doubles is to control the net. In championship-level doubles, every move is made with this end in mind. If you play beginning or intermediate-level tennis, you must necessarily be more cautious about rushing the net because you probably have less volleying ability. Nevertheless, controlling the forecourt should be your goal. Just make sure that you are coming to the net behind a strong shot.

Unlike in singles, where it is usually wise to hit the ball hard on passing shots, in doubles your best passing shot will often be a ball that is hit a little slower at one of your opponent's feet. On his return shot, he will then have to hit up to you. The ideal situation is when your opponents are hitting up and you and

CONTROLLING THE NET ... is the basic objective in doubles.

your partner are close to the net. In this position, you can hit the ball down your opponents' court, and the chances are that you will win the point.

If you are undecided about where to place your shot, keep the ball in the middle of your opponents' court. There are several reasons for doing this.

First, since there are two players on the other side, there can always be confusion about which player is going to hit the ball. This happens quite frequently with teams that have not played together often, but even with experienced teams mixups are not uncommon.

Second, if your opponents are at the net, a low shot down the middle is very effective. Even if it is returned, you will almost always be in a good position to hit the next shot. If your opponents are at the baseline and you are at the net, you should hit the ball down the middle so that they won't have a chance to pass you with a sharply angled shot. Your lobs should also be kept in the middle to minimize your opponents' angles.

A third reason for keeping the ball in the middle is that the net is a full 6 inches lower at the center than it is at the alleys. These extra inches can be particularly important in doubles, where it's to your advantage to keep the ball low.

DOUBLES STRATEGY

In planning your strategy for doubles

play, you must first realize that it is a very different game from singles. Different shots are required to be successful, and you and your partner must think and function as a team and not as two separate players.

Knowing Your Partner

The best tennis doubles partner is one whose style of play exactly complements your own. This ideal partner (and you won't get such a person very often) is able to rescue you from your own errors, set you up for your best shots, and cover your area of the court if you desert it for some reason. Since you can't always find this perfect partner, concentrate on being the perfect partner yourself. Study your teammate's game. If his backhand is strong and yours is weak, put him in the backhand court to receive the serve. If he has trouble moving around, be prepared to do a little extra running yourself. If his best shot is a smash, try to return the ball in such a way that your opponents have to hit the ball up to him.

If you have a regular partner, of course, the best way to get to know his style is to practice with him frequently. Develop a system of signals for calling balls and giving each other instructions. Work on patterns of movement until they become instinctive. Chances are your opponents won't have put in this kind of intelligent planning time, and they'll still be playing separately instead of as a unit. That will give you a tremendous advantage right from the beginning.

Mixed Doubles

These general suggestions are twice as important when you're playing mixed doubles, because the styles of the two players on a team will probably vary greatly. Most players assume that the woman will be the weaker player on the other team. That's not always true, but women do tend to play a slower game. They may compensate for their weaker serves, however, by keeping the ball in play better than men, whose most common error is to hit the ball too hard and into the net.

Frankly, the whole subject of mixed doubles makes me a bit uneasy. Many times it is impossible to separate the competition from the social aspects of the game. When a team wins, most people say it is because the woman played well; if you lose, it is because the man played badly. Sometimes a man just can't win.

A man who plays mixed doubles usually either hits at his usual pace to the man on the other side (while the two women stand there and watch), or he tries to ease up a bit and hit the ball to the other team's woman player. Either course is unsatisfactory; it throws off the timing and pace of all four players. Other men deliberately try to smash the ball at the woman. In a lot of cases, that's probably an easy way to win points. I've never been able to bring myself to do this, although I'm sure some woman players would consider that a rather condescending attitude.

The truth is, of course, that as more and more women take up tennis, a man is likely to get in serious trouble if he assumes the woman on the other team is the weaker player. We pros get a chance to watch other pros, both men and women, playing, so we can know in advance about the other players' styles. Maybe that's why tournament mixed doubles is one of the most popular tennis events for spectators. Each team has two players of widely varied playing styles, but each team works together to get the most out of the strengths and to cover for the weaknesses of each player.

For weekend tennis players, the woman usually is the weaker team member. This doesn't mean she can't compensate. One very effective shot for women to use is the lob. In competitive play the man will frequently *poach* (run over to intercept shots at the net). Often he will end up hurting his team by trying to cover too much of the court. A woman who can be counted on to hit a groundstroke properly is a much better team player than the man who tries to cover the whole court and misses his shots.

A VOLLEYING DRILL . . . with both players at the net is a good way to develop hand-eye coordination and quick reactions.

chapter 7
PRACTICE AND CONDITIONING

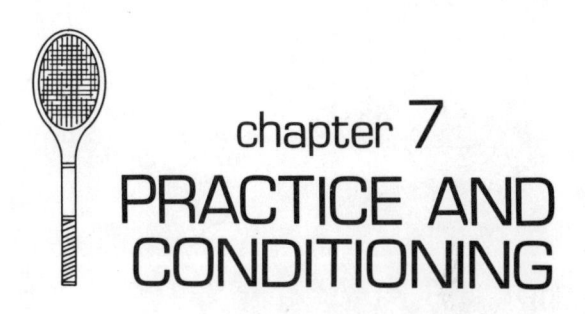

In this book I've given you advice and instruction on how to improve your game and become a strong, consistent tennis player. Important as all these instructions are, however, they won't help you much if you fail to practice regularly and keep yourself in good physical condition.

COMMONSENSE HEALTH HABITS

It goes without saying that anyone who is concerned about his health and physical conditioning will not smoke or drink. In fact, any eating or drinking habits that put strain on your body system will be detrimental to your tennis game.

Eating properly is of vital importance. Anyone who is active physically should avoid heavy, starchy foods and concentrate on a well-balanced diet that includes plenty of protein. Keep your weight down—extra weight makes each movement more difficult, slows you down, and tires you out.

Eat meals at regular hours, especially before an important match. Eat at least one to three hours before getting out on the tennis court. If the weather is hot, put some extra salt in your food.

Sleep is another important health factor. Most tournament players get between eight and nine hours of sleep consistently, but the amount varies with different individuals. The most important thing is to set a routine that you are willing to follow and with which you feel comfortable. If you are playing a match in the morning, make certain that you get up at least two and one-half hours before the match begins, so that your system will be operating at peak efficiency when it is time to play.

Always make sure that you warm up sufficiently before you practice or play. Do some general exercises and calisthenics before you subject your muscles to the rigors of intense play. Especially in cold weather, warm up very slowly so

78 PRACTICE AND CONDITIONING

A REGULAR CALISTHENICS PROGRAM... helps keep your muscles well developed. Whatever program you follow, be sure to work into the exercise gradually to avoid strained muscles.

PRACTICE AND CONDITIONING 79

LOOSEN THE ARM AND SHOULDER MUSCLES . . . by holding a couple of rackets and swinging your arm around in windmill fashion.

STRETCHING THE LEG MUSCLES...can best be accomplished by exercises such as this one.

that you don't pull or stretch any muscles.

RUNNING

As millions of people are learning, running is the best exercise for general good health and conditioning. Distance jogging is good for general body tone and for building stamina. Many professional tennis players run every day, all year long, either before or after their matches. The Davis Cup team members run regularly as part of their conditioning program.

For the serious tennis player, I recommend *wind sprints*. Warm up carefully, then run a series of 50- to 100-yard sprints, with only a few seconds of rest between each sprint. Run at your maximum energy level. If you do wind sprints every day for a few weeks, you will notice that your breathing is easier and that you are much fresher after playing two or three hard points. Be careful to build up slowly, though—you don't want any pulled muscles.

PRACTICE DRILLS

Many times players do not concentrate when they practice; consequently, they develop bad habits. I have found that using certain drills in practice makes me concentrate and develop confidence in my strokes.

Two-On-One Drill

One of the most worthwhile drills is the "two-on-one" drill. In this drill, two

PRACTICE AND CONDITIONING 81

players are either at the net or at the baseline on one side and one player in the opposite position on the other side (Diagram 20). The two players run the one from side to side and forward and backwards without stopping. If this drill is done properly, the one player should be exhausted after a few minutes.

U.S. Davis Cup Captain Dennis Ralston and former Australian Captain Harry Hopman, are both strong advocates of the two-on-one drill. The drill is a good method for pushing a player beyond his normal practice level and bringing out some of the adrenaline called for in matches.

Baseline Drill

A good drill for two players is to have

Here I am hitting the ball against the Stockman BALLBACK, a backboard that returns the ball to the same point after each stroke.

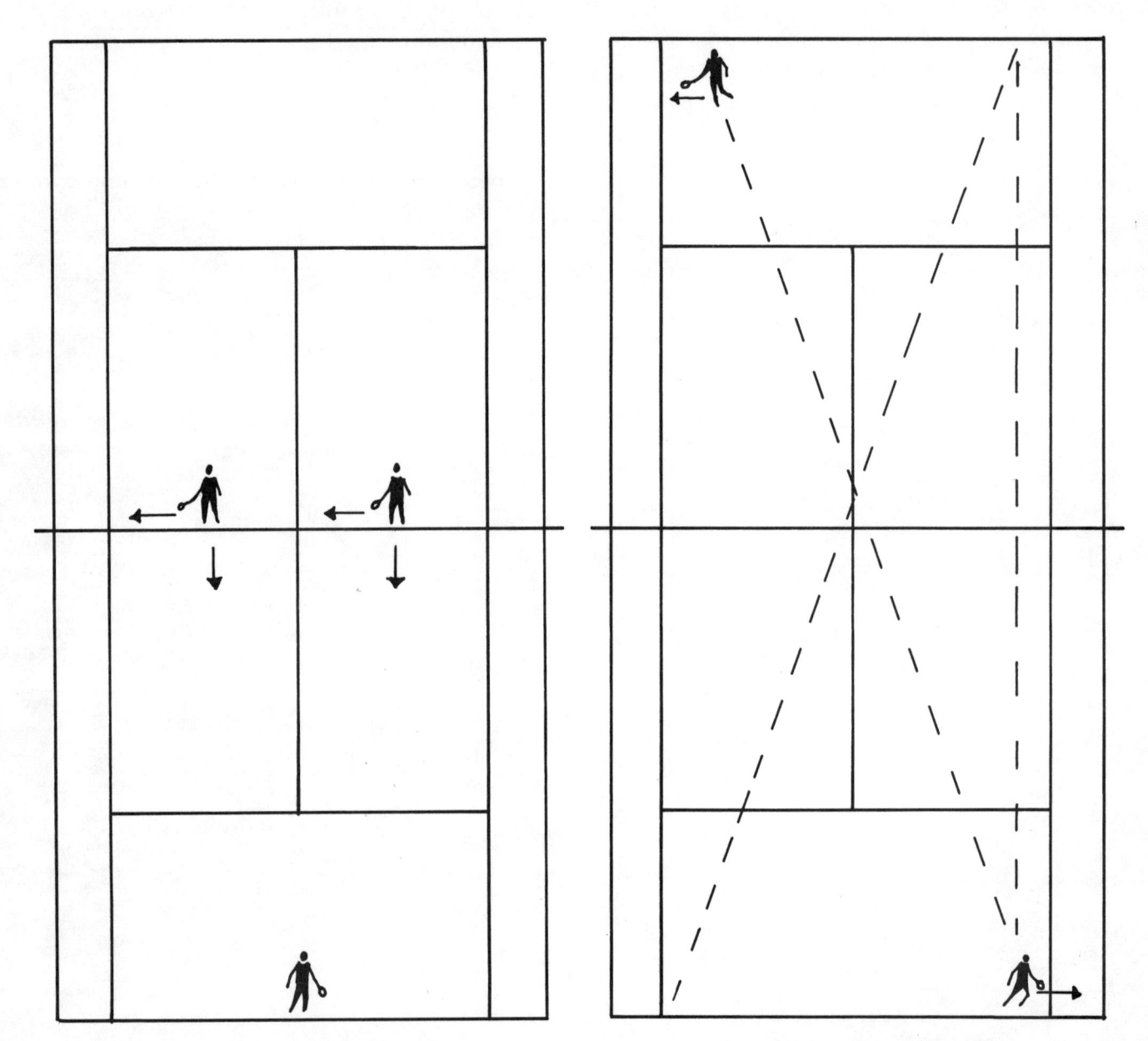

DIAGRAM 20. The two-on-one drill.

DIAGRAM 21. The baseline drill.

both players on the baseline, with one hitting cross-court and the other hitting down the line. (Diagram 21) This drill is excellent for forcing both players to run and to get their feet set in position on wide shots. After a few minutes, the players should alternate their shots. Another advantage of this drill is that it gets a player accustomed to the feel of the shots that he will need in a tight match.

Half-Court Drill

Another drill for two players uses only half the court, from the center line to doubles line (Diagram 22). In order to win points, the player at the baseline must work very hard on his lobs, chip shots, and hard passing shots. Use at least a dozen balls when doing this drill so that you don't have to stop. Only by pushing yourself can you increase your stamina in preparation for long matches.

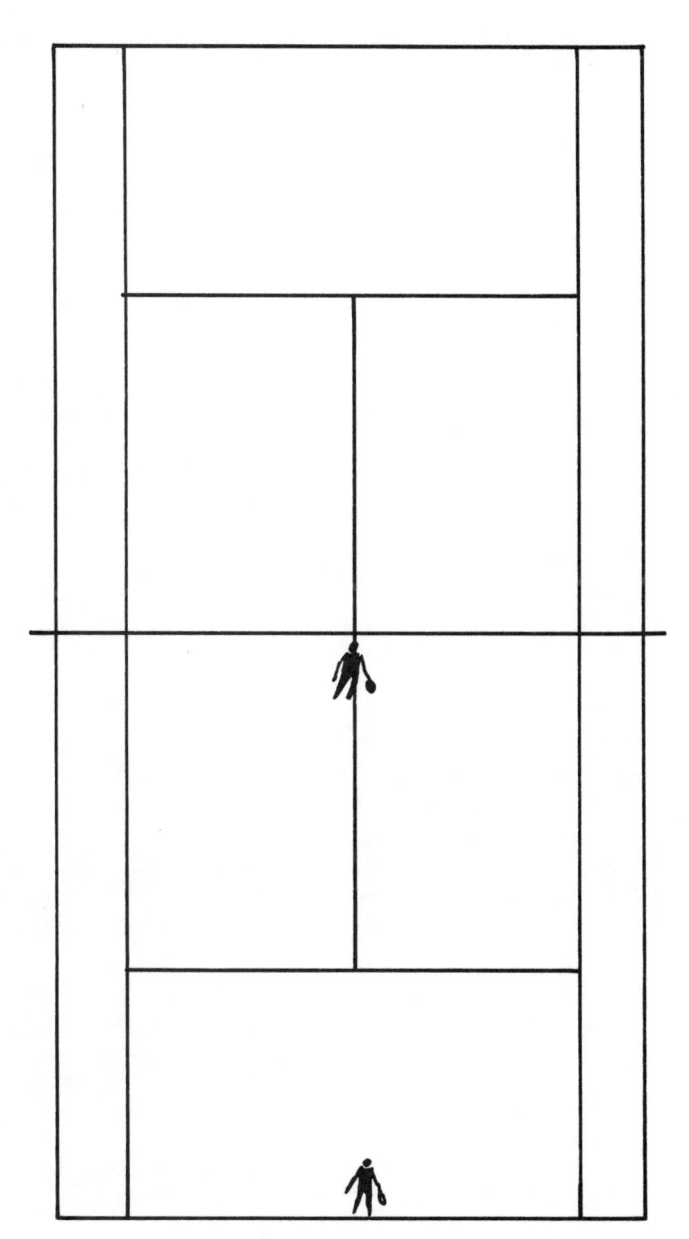

DIAGRAM 22. The half-court drill.

glossary

Ace: An unreturnable serve.

Ad: Advantage, an indication that the player needs one more point to win; the score called when the players have tied at 40-all and one player leads by one point; "ad" continues to designate any one-point lead throughout the game.

Alley: The area between the singles sidelines and the doubles sidelines. The ball may be legally hit into the alley only in doubles play.

American twist serve: An advanced serve in which the racket hits up and sideways into the ball, causing the ball to bounce high and slide into the receiver's backhand.

Approach shot: A shot hit to force the opponent back to the baseline and keep him on the defensive.

Backcourt: The area of the tennis court between the service line and the baseline. This area is 18 by 27 feet for singles and 18 by 36 feet for doubles.

Backhand: A stroke hit by right-handed players on the left side of the body and by left-handed players on the right side of the body. The racket must cross the body during the stroke.

Backhand court: The left side of the tennis court.

Backhand grip: The method of holding the racket for backhand strokes, reached by turning the racket from the forehand grip ⅛ to the left.

Baseline: The back line at either end of a tennis court.

Big game: The aggressive, attacking style of play used by most of today's leading players, which stresses rushing the net, volleying, and controlling the forecourt.

Break point: A point in which one player could possibly break the other's service, that is, win a game served by his opponent.

Center service line: The line that is perpendicular to the net, dividing the forecourt into the right and left service courts.

Continental grip: *See* Backhand grip.

Court tennis: A medieval game played by hitting a small, stuffed ball over a net; one of the forerunners of modern tennis.

Davis Cup: An annual competition consisting of teams representing more than 50 countries. Dwight Davis of the United States started the competition in 1900 between the United States and Great Britain.

Deuce: The score called when a game is tied at 40-all, and each time the score is tied throughout the rest of the game; indicates that either player needs two points to win.

Double fault: Two missed serves in a row. The server who double faults loses the point.

Drop shot: A shot in which the ball is hit barely over the net into the forecourt; usually accomplished by putting spin on the ball.

Fault: A served ball that does not strike in the proper court or is improperly served.
Flat serve: A serve in which the face of the racket hits flat against the center of the ball, causing the ball to travel in a straight line.
Foot fault: An error committed by the server if he steps over the baseline before making contact with the ball.
Forecourt: The area of the tennis court between the net and the service line. The area is 21 by 27 feet for singles and 21 by 36 feet for doubles.
Forehand: A stroke hit by right-handed players on the right side of the body and by left-handed players on the left side of the body. The racket does not cross the body during the stroke.
Forehand court: The right side of a tennis court.
Forehand grip: The method of holding the racket of forehand shots, reached by "shaking hands" with the racket. The thumb and forefinger form a "V" on top of the racket.
Forest Hills: The West Side Tennis Club in Forest Hills, New York, traditional site of the U.S. Open Championships.
Game: A unit of tennis play. A game is won by the first player to win four points by at least two, or, after a score of 4-3, to gain a lead of two points.
Grip: The handle of a tennis racket; also, the method of holding a tennis racket.
Groundstroke: A stroke hit after the ball has bounced once.
Gut: One of the materials used for stringing tennis rackets.
Half-volley: A ball hit a split-second after it has bounced, while it is still on the rise.
Head: The top of a tennis racket.
ILTF: International Lawn Tennis Federation
Let ball: A serve that touches the net and then goes into the proper court. Also, any serve that must be replayed because of outside interference.
Lob: A ball that is hit high in the air, over the head of the opposing player.
Love: Zero. A "love game" is one in which the losing player scores no points.
Match: A series of sets. Matches may consist of three or five sets.
Match point: A point that could win a match.
Mixed doubles: Doubles played by teams each consisting of one man and one woman.
Net ball: Any ball, except a serve, that hits the net and bounces to the other side. The ball continues to be in play.
Net play: Strokes, usually volleys, hit from the forecourt. Modern pro tennis concentrates on net play.
No-ad: A scoring system in which the players play only seven points, the winner being the first player to score four points.
Not up: The referee's call when a ball bounces the second time before a player reaches it. A ball that is "not up" is out of play.
Overhead: A shot used to return lobs, in which the player hits down on the ball from a point above his head in an action similar to that of serving.
Overspin serve: *See* American twist serve.
Passing shot: A ball that is hit into the backcourt past the opponent standing at the net.
Poaching: In doubles, the action of the net man in running across to his partner's side of the court to cut off a shot at the net.
Press: A frame with adjustable screws, into which a wooden tennis racket is placed to keep it from warping.
Rally: An exchange of shots from the backcourt.
Ready position: The stance assumed by a player while waiting for his opponent to return the ball.

Rushing the net: Moving to the net immediately after serving, to be in a better position for volleying.

Serve: The opening stroke of a point; the stroke that puts the ball into play.

Service court: The areas into which the ball may be hit on a serve. The two service courts, right and left, are each 13½ by 21 feet and extend from the net to the service line.

Service line: A line approximately halfway between the net and the baseline, parallel to the net.

Set: A series of games. A set is won by the first player to win six games by at least two games, or after the score of 6-5 to gain a lead of at least two games.

Short shot: A shot that lands in the forecourt (between the net and the service line).

Singles: Tennis played by two opposing players.

Slice serve: A serve in which the racket hits on the right side of the ball, causing the ball to stay low after it hits the ground and slide into the receiver's forehand.

Smash: *See* Overhead.

Sudden death: A 9-point tie breaker, in which the first player to score 5 points wins.

Throat: The spot on the tennis racket at which the handle is joined to the head.

Topspin: Spin placed on the ball when the racket comes over the ball, making it bounce forward.

Toss: The throw of the ball in the air to start the serve, or the throw of the racket in the air to determine choice of service court.

Trajectory: The angle of the ball's flight.

USLTA: United States Lawn Tennis Association.

VASSS: Van Alen Simplified Scoring System.

Volley: A stroke made by hitting the ball before it has touched the ground, except on a serve.

WCT: World Championship of Tennis, a major tennis circuit in which most of the top male pros compete.

Wimbledon: The site of the British Open, the world's most prestigious tennis tournament.

index

Adjusting to playing conditions, 65-67
Advantage, 11
Alley, 5
Amateur vs. pro controversy, 2
American twist serve, 24-25
Analysis
  of doubles partner, 74
  of one's own game, 61-62
  of opponent's game, 63
Anticipation, 63
Approach shots, 46-48
Astroturf, 6

Backcourt, 5, 31, 63
Backhand, 26, 27, 31, 35-41, 43
  on approach shots, 48
  on volleys, 53-54
    See also Grip; names of individual strokes
Backswing. See names of individual strokes
Balls, 8-9
Baseline drill, 81
"Big game," 31

Cement courts, 6
Clay courts, 6, 66
Clothing, 9-10
Concrete courts, 6, 66
Conditioning, 77-83
Conduct, 12-13
Confidence, 25, 29
Connors, Jimmy, 41
Continental grip, 18
Court(s)
  dimensions of, 5-6
  surfaces of, 5, 47
Court tennis, 1
Crosscourt shots, 15, 48

Davis Cup, 1, 81
Davis, Dwight, 1
Defense against lobs, 57
Defensive lobs, 56
Dell, Dick, 11
Deuce, 11
Double fault, 15
Doubles, 5, 69-75

Drop shot(s), 50, 54-55
Drysdale, Cliff, 41
Dynaturf, 6
Eastern grip. See Grip, forehand
Equipment, 7-10
Evert, Chris, 27
Evert, Jeanne, 27

Fault, 15
15-30-40-game, 11
First serve, 28
Flat backhand, 36-37
Flat serve, 15, 22-23
Following serve to net, 44-46
Follow-through
  on approach shots, 48
  on backhand, 37, 38
  on drop shots, 54-55
  on forehand, 35
  on half-volleys, 54
  on serves, 20-21, 45
  on volleys, 53-54
Foot fault, 15
Forecourt, 5, 63
Forehand, 31, 32-35, 43
  approach shots, 47-48
  grip for, 16
  on volleys, 53

Grip
  in ready position, 44
  of racket, 8
  on backhand, 35-36
  on forehand, 32
  on smash, 56
  on volleys, 53
Grass courts, 5-6, 65
Grasstex, 6
Groundstrokes, 31-41, 45
Gut, 8

Half-court drill, 83
Half-volley, 50, 54
Head (or racket), 8
Health habits, 77
Heat, adjusting for, 10, 67

Lawn tennis, 1
Laykold, 6
Leach, Dick, 11
Let ball, 15
Lob(s), 48, 50, 55-56
Longwood Cricket Club, 7
Love, 11
Lutz, Bob, 69

Match, 11
Mixed doubles, 74
Mozur, Tom, 11

Net play, 31
 in doubles, 72-73
Newport Casino, 1
No-ad scoring, 12

Offensive lob(s), 55
Open tennis, 2
Older players, 62
Overhead, 50, 56-59
Overspin serve. *See* American twist serve

Passing shots, 48
Percentage tennis, 25
Placement of serves, 27-28
Plexipave, 6
Poaching, 75
Point of contact on serve, 20
Practice drills, 80-83
Press, 8

Rackets, 7-8
Ralston, Dennis, 81
Ready position, 31
Receiving order for doubles, 70
Return of serve, 43-44
 in doubles, 72
Rosewall, Ken, 27, 29
Rules, 5, 10-11
 changes in, 2
 for doubles, 69-71
 for serving, 15
Rushing the net, 45

Schloss, Len, 11
Scoring, 10-12
Second serve, 29
Segura, Pancho, 2
Serve, 10, 15-29
 in doubles, 71-72
Service courts, 5
Set, 10, 11
Short shot, 47
Singles, 5
Slice backhand, 37-38
Slice serve, 15, 23-24
Smash. *See* Overhead
Spin, 19, 24, 25
Sportface, 6
Sportsmanship, 12-13
Stance for serving, 18
Strategy, 58, 61-67
 for serving, 25-29
 in doubles, 73-75
  See also names of individual strokes
Stringing the racket, 8
Sudden Death, 11
Sun, adjusting for, 66-67
Swing (on serve), 19-20
Synthetic courts, 6

Tennis Court Oath, 1
Tennis history, 1-2
Television coverage, 1, 11
Throat of racket, 8
Tie-breakers, 11
Topspin, 34, 55, 56
Topspin backhand, 37
Toss
 on American twist serve, 24
 on serves, 18-19, 45
 on slice serve, 23
Trajectory of ball, 64
"Trigger action" of wrist, 20
Two-handed backhand, 41
Two-on-one drill, 80

Underspin, 55
United States Lawn Tennis Association, 5

Van Alen, James Henry, 11
Variety of strokes, 64
VASSS, 11-12
Virginia Slims Circuit, 2
Volley(s), 31, 50-55

Warm-up, 77
Weight of racket, 8

Wimbledon, 1
Wind, adjusting for, 66
Wind sprints, 80
Wingfield, Major Walter, 1
Women's pro tennis, 2
World Championship of Tennis, 11
World Tennis magazine, 2